T0344412

Michael Jakob
Faux Mountains

EDITIONS

Publishers of Architecture, Art, and Design
Gordon Goff: Publisher

www.oroeditions.com
info@oroeditions.com

Published by ORO Editions

Graphic Design: Michael and Isabel Jakob
Text: Michael Jakob
Translation: Désirée Morales Ruiz
Project Coordinator: Jake Anderson

10 9 8 7 6 5 4 3 2 1 First Edition

Library of Congress data available upon request.

ISBN: 978-1-943532-55-1

Color Separations and Printing: ORO Group Ltd.
Printed in China.

International Distribution: www.oroeditions.com/distribution

ORO Editions makes a continuous effort to minimize the overall carbon footprint of its
publications. As part of this goal, ORO Editions, in association with Global ReLeaf, arranges
to plant trees to replace those used in the manufacturing of the paper produced for its books.
Global ReLeaf is an international campaign run by American Forests, one of the world's oldest
nonprofit conservation organizations. Global ReLeaf is American Forests' education and
action program that helps individuals, organizations, agencies, and corporations improve the
local and global environment by planting and caring for trees.

Why is there something rather than nothing?

—Martin Heidegger

1

Foreword

Our study offers a critical analysis of a phenomenon that has almost entirely escaped the gaze of history while not being rare or exceptional. The false mountain, an accumulation of material in an artificial form that resembles a real mountain, opens up a vast diachronic and geographical field. To gather into one book the mountains, or built mounds that call out to us, is equivalent to probing their intelligibility. In our opinion, these objects make sense: as a pile, heap, or mound, they contain the most diverse materials (which also require analysis) while accumulating the complex processes, gestures, and activities that generated them. Our intention is to let these more or less massive, more or less visible artifacts "speak." Convinced as we are that beneath their surface, and behind their form, lie buried treasures of intelligence.

It goes without saying that the Parnassus built during the Renaissance has been the medium of messages and a prerequisite for a certain type of *architecture parlante*. To define a mound of a few meters in height in the style of the Parnassus does not provide all its merit; it asks for an explanation that reveals the meaning of this carefully composed sign. Moreover, whenever a new Parnassus emerges, its reiteration in other contexts exposes us to a relation of identity and difference, whereby the new constructions take up or surpass the previous ones. The multiplied and disseminated Parnassus quotes, copies, repeats, cancels or, on the contrary, outclasses its models. Yet the entirety of these cumbersome signifiers leading to the shape of the artificial mountain does not shed any light on the respective sense, i.e., the specific stake of these creations. Indeed, what is hidden behind the symbol of Parnassus, reincarnated in gardens in Italy or France, far from its native Greece? Why is a heap of earth, covered here and there by a green layer, a mound adorned with antique or antiquarian statues, presented as a Parnassus? And, why such an effort at all? Other objects which took the shape of the mountain built from scratch, such as the architectural mountain of the Revolution, immediately fall within the framework of a semiotic operation calling for a double reception—individual and collective. The presence of the Mountains of the Revolution in the context of the celebrations of the Supreme Being also refers, in any case, to a particular hermeneutic horizon which implies a major imaginative investment by the receiver. Within these large-scale projects, one did not only move and compress material—one also stacked elements or strata which, as a whole, had to provide meaning. Other artifacts in our directory do not bear significance at first glance: they are hidden from view or remain "neutral," such as most of the heaps or mountains of waste to which our gaze has fixated over the centuries. Even where these eminences stemming from industrial activity or energy production flows continue to be erected, they are almost completely ignored by us. And yet, these objects are quite there; they occupy and mark the ground, confer a character or topography to a site, and they form the artificial perimeter of a radically anthropomorphic landscape.

Should we probe the genesis of these great, silent signs scattered over the earth's surface, or do we also add one more anthropomorphic gesture to their appearance by taking an interest in them? Although these mounds are the result, with no exception, of a prior constructive activity, the inaugural act and the "plan" which gave rise to them, often differ from one type to another. There are artificial mountains designed with art, projected down to the smallest detail, while others, equally imposing, seem to appear randomly, or rise up from the ground, without anyone knowing why. These give themselves, at least initially, as a negligible supplement to more important activities. The link to something else—always found in the context of artificial mountains—is an essential data. It implies that any such construction belongs to a system that goes beyond or encompasses it, even in cases where the artifact itself is already monumental in its own right. The faux mountain is, therefore, never what it is on its own. Its existence refers to an activity that precedes it, an action often comparable in size and complexity to the evident result. In short, these human-made mounds are never purely decorative, and one only has to enumerate a few concepts closely defining them to realize it.

An obvious first link exists between artificial mountains and vertical constructions in the classical sense of the term, i.e. architectural objects. Raising a mountain to a certain height requires structural skills and knowledge of materials. No false mountain without *firmitas*. From substruction work to shaping, the implemented processes are similar; from "primitive" architectures such as "vegetal huts" or "mud huts," to mound tombs, and right up to the Tower of Babel, designed to reinstate the ancient earth-sky axis shattered by the Flood. It is difficult to separate what belongs to the mountain form and what belongs to the architectural form. As a stacked mass, compacted material, structured assembly, tower, cathedral, or skyscraper, architecture is similar to the mountain's formation. The proximity becomes evident in the analogy between Gaudí's *Sagrada Família* and *Montserrat*, the isolated massif of Catalonia known for its jagged outline. In the context of the extreme density of large cities, the daring constructions that soar toward the sky form a similar mountain chain.

All of this has already become clear in Giovanni Battista Piranesi's fantastic visions. The Venetian architect and artist likes to stage both the ruins of the

TOP LEFT AND RIGHT Antoni Gaudí, *Sagrada Família*, drawing, 1910
BOTTOM Giovanni Battista Piranesi, *Veduta di un gran masso...*, etching,
in: *Le Antichità Romane*, vol. III, plate XV, Rome 1756

A

B

VEDUTA di un gran Masso, Avanzo del Sepolcro della Famiglia de Metelli sulla Via Appia cinque miglia in circa fuori di Porta S. Sebastiano nel Casale di S. Maria Nuova. Questo nobile Sepolcro fu spogliato non solamente de suoi più magnifici ornamenti, ma ancora d'ogni altro marmo, che lo copriva, e fu talmente scavato all'intorno nella parte di sotto presso terra, che sembra miracolo a vedersi come possa sussistere quasi affatto per aria una mole sì grande. A Avanzo di muro reticolato, il quale può credersi, che servisse di recinto alla Villa de Metelli, dentro la quale era fabbricato il Sepolcro, acciocchè fosse meglio custodito. B Altri Avanzi de Sepolcri.

Piranesi Archit dis dil.

past, over-emphasizing their cumulative appearance as solitary peaks occupying the landscape, and displaying all the enormous masses laid out like a row of mountains. Mountain building refers to an idea of verticality found, of course, in the concept of mountain itself and also in the primordial architectural act on which all building activity is based. Referring to the etymology of the noun *pays* ("land" in French)—derived from the Latin verb *pango*: I drive a stake, a stick into the ground[1]—we can assert a symbolic occupation of the land by the gesture of the hand pushing a vertical element into the earth throughout the centuries, from the great pyramids and tumuli to cathedrals, baroque towers and modern skyscrapers.

Erecting a mountain using solid materials establishes a relationship with Nature. The stone, the rock, and the mound represent in a microcosm what Nature has built on a large scale. This "as if" of the artificial mountain acquires divergent meanings according to the different and specific realizations. During the Renaissance, the mountain as a hyper-visible artifact followed the poetics of imitation that became canonical with Aristotle, a mimetic process marking all artistic activities. During the Revolution, the exhibition of a grandiose architectural mountain in a celebratory context marked—in contrast—the return to a natural state as the symbolic advent of a new order. And what about Prince Herrmann von Pückler-Muskau, who, after building two pyramids, a dual gigantic folly, in his garden in Branitz, had himself buried in one of them? Did he rediscover through this exceptional location an eternity typical of real mountains?

In a more secular version, the Great Rock of the Vincennes Zoo, a true masterpiece of early twentieth-century construction technology, also exhibits the connection to Nature; however, the modern human being—an engineer capable of manufacturing Nature—does not limit itself to displaying abilities, since he masters its construction from a structural aspect. The relation to Nature, with the mountain as one of its possible metonymies, is never an abstract data; rather, it appears as a fundamental part of the project in question, which implies that the meaning of the mountain as an element imitating Nature is different every time. Our artifact imitating nature can thus be the bearer of various messages, the essence of which lies within the fact that it always signifies a "surplus" already embodied by its size.

The significant quality of the artificial mountains we intend to examine requires particular attention to a figure of style and an aesthetic sign of the highest order: the symbol. To question artificial mountains is equivalent to questioning the symbol. The word, derived from the Greek term *synballein* (συμβάλλειν) meaning "to put, carry, throw together," implies a kind of implosion, that scattered elements are compressed into a single central element, a symbol. The objects we are going to analyze all obey the logic of the symbol. They impose themselves as a sign that occupies the ground, crushing all that surrounds it, a seemingly self-sufficient object that prevails over any other visible element. The artifacts of interest here are indeed all related to ideas. They symbolize an abstract meaning that prevailed when they were created. The tinkered mountain, which imposes itself on the view from afar, acts as a visual reminder of what normally eludes representation. With the characteristic that the shape of the material sign and the idea it is representing maintain a link of resemblance. Artificial mounts, often of considerable size, thus appear to be the significant product of the symbol-making subject; an animal *symbolicum* according to Ernst Cassirer. For example, the mounds erected in Renaissance gardens are much more than piles of earth; they are Parnassus, the symbolic remake of an antique model with everything that this mythical place implies. Baroque mounds, most often built as ephemeral architecture, constitute the visible side of an allegorical staging in which the mountain (Parnassus, Helicon or Olympus) assumes a meaning in the broader context of political discourse. Tectonically shaped artifacts in 20th century works of landscape architecture, seemingly purely formal at first glance, also tell the story of a transformation of the earth, as well as the price to pay for this type of intervention.

This "message" conveyed by the man-made mountain is all the more evident within the context of Renaissance projects. The idea of Renaissance, which appeared for the first time in Vasari's *Lives* (*Vite*), aims at a global revival based on the discovery of antiquity's knowledge. However, building a mountain using remains buried in the earth, or decorating a mound with statues, also taken from the ground, appears to be the perfect representation of the processes put into action during the historical phase called "rebirth." The symbolic gesture of the Renaissance thus begins as a rediscovery of what is hidden underground.[2] It is an archaeological act, which mixes melancholy (due to the discovery of the remains of a dead civilization) and the pleasure of finding seemingly precious fragments of the past. The Renaissance essentially digs; it reaches down into the bowels of the earth, it penetrates space and time, extracting from the earth a sort of enormous hole or reverse mountain, the remains with which it intends, here and now, to build the future. Brunelleschi and Alberti, among the most illustrious representatives of that time, began their career by digging, analyzing, and collecting, in a literal way, the remains of the past. The gaping holes of ancient Rome are hidden treasures, but also an enormous mass of materials that will be used for renovation. The new

Pietro da Cortona, *Mount Athos being cut to resemble a giant with a waterfall forming from his hands*, engraving and etching, ca 1657-1681

perspective on antiquity, the awakening, the curiosity for "buried" things, followed by building activities in all fields of culture have symbolically shaped the artificial mountains that adorn the most important gardens of the time, gardens which are based as well on antique references. The radical metamorphosis of the heteronomous human being into an autonomous subject; the elevation of the educated and proud human being, the possibility of escaping from a closed world, and the claim to open space seen from the top of a peak as a projective horizon—all these aspects are reflected in the architectural mountains which, like new Parnassus, relate the triumph of an extraordinary act of refoundation. Whether during the Renaissance, the Baroque period, or the Great Revolution, the mountainous form, staged with considerable means, has become the hyper-visible affirmation of a large-scale semiotic operation.[3]

1   See Catherine Franceschi, "Du mot paysage et ses équivalents en cinq langues européennes," in: *Les enjeux du paysage*, ed. Michel Collot, Ousia, Bruxelles 1997, pp. 75-111.

2   See Thomas M. Greene, *The Light in Troy, Imitation and Discovery in Renaissance Poetry*, Yale University Press, New Haven 2016.

3   On the theme of artificial mountains in general, see Michael Jakob, "On Mountains: scalable and unscalable," in: *Landform Building. Architecture's new Terrain*, ed. Stan Allen, Marc McQuade, Lars Müller, Zurich 2011, pp. 136-164; *Felsengärten, Gartengrotten, Kunstberge: Motive der Natur in Architektur und Garten*, ed. Uta Hassler, Hirmer, Munich 2014; *Konstruierte Bergerlebnisse*, ed. Uta Hassler, Hirmer, Munich 2015; Claire Portal, "The artificial mountain: a new articulated form of nature?," in: *Revue de géographie alpine* 105-2 (2017), online.

ABOVE Romeyne de Hooghe, *Aangezicht op de berg van Parnas*, engraving on copper, ca 1685

2

The Renaissance of Parnassus

The wedding ceremony of Costanzo Sforza and Camilla d'Aragona in 1475, at Pesaro, in the Marches, was accompanied by a festive procession celebrating the *Santa Poesia*. This celebration, which lasted several days, brought together a set of mythological elements with triumphal chariots that displayed, among others, the seven planets, an Orpheus, and an allegory of Poetry. One of the main elements of the procession was a Sugar Parnassus, carried by three allegorical figures—Grammar, Rhetoric, and Astrology—and ceremoniously entrusted to the spouses. An illustration of the period[1] shows in addition to these three female figures, the mountain, the nine muses, Apollo, and his lyre, a laurel tree and a fountain. The miniature Parnassus was followed by ten Greek and ten Latin poets, dressed in precious clothing, walking next to each other, and holding a book also made of sugar. "Poetry" presented the miniature Parnassus to the couple, reciting a poem in Latin and Italian. At the same time she explained the meaning of the symbol:

> Since the fame of your triumph
> Sprinkled with trophies came to the sacred mount
> Where the one who covets virtue is sitting, immortal
> The Muses and Phebus were ready with me
> To visit your excellence
> With this mixture of disorder and care
> Here is the Parnassus and the beautiful spring on which
> Of all doctrines the spirit is fed
> And the breasts of those ascending it.[2]

This ephemeral parade is both a point of arrival and departure. On one hand, it represents the consecration of an ancient place which, from rough, wild and distant mountains, has been able to metamorphose into its opposite, namely a sacred nature with an idyllic aspect and synonymous with Apollonian inspiration. On the other hand, it also marks the beginning of the fortunes of the artificial mountains such as Mount Parnassus in the great gardens of the Renaissance.[3] Among the Greeks, Parnassus was, in principle, only a minor mountain—one among others. It was only gradually, and especially during the transition from Greek to Roman culture, that it enjoyed a remarkable success and increase importance as time passed, with the Renaissance marking the peak of its evolution. The proximity of Delphi, the most venerated religious place of ancient Greece, had already contributed to its "apollonization" as

well as its attachment, during the Roman period, to the "world's navel."[4] Originally associated with Dionysus and his extravagances, the famous mountain with its two peaks will be shared for a time by the complementary couple, Dionysus and Apollo (see Pausanias X, 4, 3). In Rome, particularly after the battle of Actium (in 31 BCE), Mount Parnassus became one of the symbols of Apollo, and a symbol of victory made possible by his intervention (see Pliny, H. N., XV, chap. 29, 133-135). It is, however, the confusion created by the Roman poet Statius that will lay the basis for its subsequent true valorization. The Latin author mixes elements related to Mount Parnassus with features of Helicon, the other sacred mountain of Apollo much lower and gentler, identified by Hesiod as the mountain of the Muses. By transposing the Muses and Pegasus as well as the famous Hippocrene spring on Parnassus, Statius and his successors established the concept of an exemplary mountain, synonymous with inspiration and eternal glory. Confusion between the two mountains is present in the commentary on the *Aeneid* by Servius (commentary to *Aen.* VII, 641), a text that will leave its mark well beyond the Middle Ages. Henceforth, and for more than a millennium, Parnassus was *the* sacred and poetic mountain. Having lost its wild connotation, it appears as a kind of earthly paradise, endowed with a spring and magical qualities. Antiquity has become familiar with the image of the poetic encounter on the Parnassus, which is essential in the context of its rediscovery during the Renaissance. Thus, Lucretius says that the Roman poet Ennius met Homer in a dream at the Parnassus, who initiated him to the "secrets of being" and reincarnated himself as the Latin poet.[5]

The subsequent amplification of Parnassus occurred paradoxically at a time when the difference between the mountain and the Helicon became once again evident. It had been Boccaccio in his *Genealogia deorum gentilium* who set things straight based on geographical arguments. Both Dante and Petrarch related to Parnassus: the former at the invocation of Apollo in Paradise (*Par.* I, 13-46), the latter in the context of his coronation speech of 1341, which symbolically begins with a quotation from Virgil: *sed me Parnasi deserta per ardua dulcis ruptat amor* ("But a sweet love takes me along the deserted slopes of Parnassus," *Georg.* II, vv. 289-293). For the author of the *Canzoniere*, the Parnassus becomes the heavenly scene for a prospective imagination that allows dialogue between the masters of Antiquity and those of the modern era. His coronation speech held in Rome started with the idea of an abandoned and ruined Parnassus, eventually reconquered by modern culture. By accomplishing the arduous ascent of the exemplary mountain, the poet of Laura expresses his willingness to "climb" as high as his ancient predecessors. Petrarch intends to give new life to poetry, the first among all arts at the time, which is equivalent to winning the laurel wreath (the last poet recognized was Statius).

The image of the Parnassus omnipresent in the work of Petrarch increased in importance from his establishment in Fontaine de Vaucluse in 1337. This haven of peace and place of inspiration was immediately identified by Petrarch as *mons Parnaso* or *Helicon*. Here, where he wrote his *Scattered Rimes* (or *Song Book, Canzoniere*), but also the epic *Africa*, he built two gardens. One was dedicated to Apollo, the other to Dionysus, thus resuming the duality of the two-headed mountain, half Apollonian, half Dionysiac. It is here, in the beloved solitude of the Vaucluse that he will "live," according to his own words, in the immediate company of the authors of Antiquity. Within his little Parnassus, he will talk incessantly with the masters of the past; he will treat them as guests and as true friends, friends by the names Horace, Virgil, Cicero, Seneca, or Titus Livius. Here, in the heart of the Vaucluse, he identified the early signs of the renewal of times: "And now we begin to see again the double-crested Helicon and the spring born from the horse's hoof and the green forest of the poets and a brighter fate smiling at the wretched."[6]

The idea of closeness with his "great friends," actualized as physical contact with his illustrious colleagues of the past and practiced in his new transalpine Parnassus, favors a timeless conception of the mythical place. This timeless Parnassus, exclusively reserved for those worthy of Apollo's crown, allowed to transpose the glorious past into the present and to imagine another, more radiant future. In his epic *Africa*, the poet imagined the advent of a new era by resorting to the mythical mountain and, in particular, by relying on the syncretic Parnassus-Heliconian scheme: "Then on the Helicon you will see a new tree appear and the sacred laurels cover themselves with leaves; Then high spirits and docile souls will arise for whom the passion for good will redouble the ancient love of the Muses."[7]

The *Triumphs of Petrarch* (and above all, the *Trionfo della Fama*, the *Triumph of Fame*) only strengthened the centrality of Parnassus in the Renaissance culture. It is precisely this work that served as a model for countless festive ceremonies in the following centuries. The example of Petrarch, imitated by

TOP RIGHT Francesco Petrarca, drawing, in: Plinius the Elder, *Historia Naturalis* (Bibl. vat. lat. 6802, f. 143v)

a large number of minor authors, provided the conceptual basis for the resurgence of Parnassus in all fields of art, whether literary or artistic, ephemeral, or enduring. The transfer from the literary and the immaterial plan to the concreteness of an on site installation, that is to say the construction of a new Parnassus in miniature, begins in Ferrara. In 1471, the year of his death, Borso d'Este, Duke of Ferrara, undertook fortification work that would be continued by several of his successors well into the 16th century. In a short period of time, Ferrara, a city with an unfortunate topography due to excessive exposure to its enemies because of its location on an open plain, developed a highly original defense system. It is, indeed, a skillful mix of bastions and gardens that will characterize the redesigned urban territory, with a vast hunting estate (*barco*) as a landmark, a green space that was used for agriculture, hunting, and recreation (it was even equipped with a maze for horse racing). In this context, the garden was of strategic and programmatic interest. It allowed to "sneak out or enter the city, to accomplish real escapes, to discreetly receive illustrious guests or, on the contrary, to pompously welcome ranking visitors."[8] On the symbolic level, it appeared as the crowning of an attempt by man to control Nature, in short, as the triumph of artifice: "artificial climates are created, land is shaped in improbable ways, the waters of the Po River are manipulated by complex hydraulic interventions."[9]

The fortification works under Borso d'Este already led to the accumulation of materials and later, to the construction of several mounds: the so called *montagnone*, to the northeast of the fortifications; the one known as Saint-Georges' mountain, to the southeast, and another construction that has now disappeared, to the west. These large mounds, directly connected to the fortification works in progress, are therefore the result of the accumulation of residual material. They were called *cavalieri* (literally knights) and were used as defensive platforms to counter enemy attacks with cannons.[10] Assembled in a landscaped area and carefully constructed, they immediately acquired a specific meaning: they were majestic artificial objects that caught the eye and demanded to be invested with a meaning. In other words, they had to be included in a narrative framework. However, initially, before disappearing behind the somewhat banal designation of *montagnole* or before being Christianized, the mounds of Ferrara were miniature Parnassus.

This is a historical period when Parnassus was omnipresent in Ferrara. It can be seen in several images of the famous "calendar" of Schifanoia, a residence located a few steps from the mountain of Saint George. We know that in 1470, three of the representations of the cycle had already been realized. In the picture representing the month of May, one can easily recognize the mountain with the two peaks—Apollo and the Muses—the Hippocrene spring, the triumphal chariot, all the topical elements of a Parnassus that occupies the forefront in the poetry, painting, music and "applied arts" of Northern Italy. It can also be found at the same period in Andrea Mantegna's *Parnassus*, likely made for the *Studiolo* of Isabella d'Este in Mantua around 1490. The famous painting, now in the Louvre, shows on the right the double-peaked

---

ABOVE Andrea Mantegna, *Le Parnasse* (Parnaso), 1497, Louvre

mountain, with a water source in the middle, the rocky mass pierced every-where by a series of caves, not forgetting Pegasus the winged horse. The presence of these caves is at first sight surprising. Why is the mythical mountain so hollow? The answer can be found in Strabo's *Geography*, a book translated and published in 1472 in Venice (Mantegna worked on the composition of the initials of this Strabo edition). The ancient geographer, who has just been rediscovered by humanists, formulated it very clearly:

> The entire region of Parnassus is considered to be devoted to Apollo, as there are caves and other places that are honored and considered sacred. The most famous and most beautiful of them is Korykion, a cave of the nymph with the same name as the one in Kilikia.[11]

A testimony from 1671 clearly associates one of the mountains of Ferrara to this tradition of the Parnassus with caves:

> To the left of the said labyrinth was the aforementioned mountain, made by hand, above two vaulted rooms that looked like caves, the inside of which was square, not very large, decorated with mosaics and decorated in relief with grotesques and arabesques nicely colored and gilded; the other room, much larger and round in shape, also decorated with several niches and paintings, also gilded [...] and this mountain, not natural, but built by man [...] one climbs it by two more or less opposite paths, covered with various pergolas with exquisite grapes, and which continued all around the square, where the highest part of the said Mountain ended, which served not only to please the eye, embracing the whole city and the neighboring country, but also as a knight ready to defend the city itself.[12]

Let us retain here several characteristics of this remarkable artificial mountain, carefully composed in the manner of a complex work of art. It is a precious artifact, due to its spectacular interior, while the more natural exterior is partly covered by vines and shrubs. This strange object concentrates on a single construction two aspects that the Sienese architect Francesco di Giorgio Martini had programmatically separated in his project for a large octagonal *barco*. Within the latter, a regular and purely geometrical mound is topped by a generous circular pavilion. This central place, which attracts all the attention and which would have allowed the visual control of the surrounding space from a high point of view, was a response to a second, opposite construction. A small mountain planted with trees indeed represented the "natural" model diverted and surpassed by the central mound.

However, in the *montagnetta* of Ferrara, reduced around 1611 to half its size, these two functions had been brought together and gave rise to a plural work that skillfully plays with the oppositions of nature vs. artifice, outside vs. inside, full vs. empty. This new typology, which can also be found in Pratolino, near Florence, reminds us of mytho-poetic notions (the *Hell* of the Dantesque *Comedy* as a "negative" funnel in opposition to the "positive" form of the mountain of

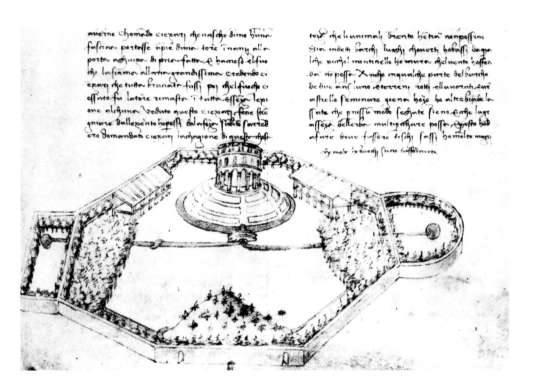

ABOVE Francesco di Giorgio Martino, Codex Saluzziano 148, *Trattato di architettura civile e militare*, Bibl. Reale, Turin, ca 1470

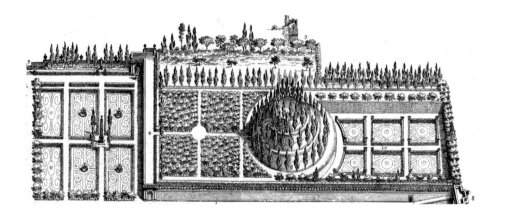

Purgatory and *Paradise*) as well as systemic considerations behind a construction of this type. In order to erect an elevated object in Ferrara, one had to dig first, which is done in parallel with the tinkering of ancient literary pieces in modern texts. But digging, on a temporal level, is equivalent to going back to the glorious past of antiquity. The reborn Parnassus, resulting from the scattered fragments of ancient civilization, owes its existence to an "archaeological" operation.

The construction details of the artificial mountains of Ferrara and those that will follow are lacking. It would be valuable to get more information on the projects as such, on the technical, static, ornamental, and aesthetic aspects. Above all, the role of intellectuals—poets such as Prisciano Pellegrini, who had followed the Schifanoia cycle construction site—should be taken into consideration when drawing up the programs underlying these ambitious projects. It would also be useful to find more precise information about the design of mounds during the great festivals of the period, such as that of Padua in 1466, known mainly by the famous wooden horse built by Donatello. Or in 1490, in Milan, the mountain on the stage that Lodovico il Moro had commissioned from Leonardo da Vinci for the *Festa del Paradiso*. Same goes for the mountain made during the performance of Plautus's comedy *Menaechmi*, at Ferrara, in February 1491, this time as part of another grandiose wedding (Alfonso d'Este and Anna Sforza). Did Apollo, followed by the nine Muses who praised the bride and groom, also appear on the summit of a Parnassus? Other questions regarding the genesis of the Parnassus model built from scratch arise in the light of the first Roman or Tuscan sculpture gardens. Isn't it logical that, in a generous garden adorned with statues barely pulled out of the ground, a skillfully arranged mound could serve as a spatial and conceptual framework taking precisely the form and identity of a reborn Parnassus?[13]

All these threads converge in the Parnassus as a symbol, bringing together the key ideas of the time. It is Parnassus as a mountain to be climbed laboriously and a major symbol of renewal, initiated by the generation of Dante,

---

Petrarch, Boccaccio, and pursued by the humanists of the following century, that expresses the pride and positioning of the new *homo faber*: a modern subject who rises, ascends and demonstratively occupies a totalizing point of view; a summit made possible by the construction of a platform imitating both Nature and the exemplary Antiquity.

Once the Parnassus' multi-medial installation was consolidated (including poetry, painting, sculpture, architecture, and music), it was quickly taken up in a large number of 16th-century gardens. Parnassus will be built in Rome in the Giardino del Bufalo, Villa Madama, Villa Mattei, and the Casino Pius IV, but also in the two Este villas in Tivoli and Rome, Villa Aldobrandini, Villa Lante in Bagnaia and, in the same region, in Bomarzo. The famous Villa d'Este in Tivoli, with its garden created in the 1560s, is a logical extension of the Ferrara experience. The Pegasus Fountain, set on a Parnassus rock, was best known for its crystal-clear water—an act of *sprezzatura* due to the massive use of the precious liquid for purely aesthetic reasons. One of the highlights of these increasingly imposing Parnassus was on the Pincio, the hill of the gardens of Antiquity, in the estate of Villa Medici. Built at the initiative of Cardinal Ferdinando de Medici, in 1576, this 14-meter high *montagnetta* occupied, or rather encompassed within itself the remains of a *nymphaeum* and two ancient temples (the *nymphaeum* was a large fountain dedicated to the cult of aquatic deities). A cave led into the bowels of the glorious past, while outside a tiered conical structure adorned with cypress trees moved from Gaeta in 1573 led visitors upwards. Following the sixty or so steps, one reached a summit which, as in Ferrara, allowed one to embrace the spectacle of the eternal city from a truly privileged point of view. The shape chosen for this artificial mountain was reminiscent of a mausoleum and linked the new construction to the great funerary remains of Augustus and Hadrian, conferring a sublime solemnity to the complex. With the Villa Medici mountain-mausoleum (the use of water was also truly superlative and pumped from 50 meters above) the water from the Acqua Vergine—the source of water recently re-established after an interruption of almost a millennium—generously irrigated the grandiose composition.

In the same years, another Medici garden was created in Pratolino, Tuscany, an estate that also boasted a Parnassus and was greatly admired by contemporaries. This

BOTTOM RIGHT Giovanni Guerra, *Monte Parnaso*, Pratolino, ca 1598, Albertina, Vienna

artificial mountain was covered with laurels and adorned with statues of Apollo, the Muses, and a Pegasus flying into the heavens. A hydraulic organ, hidden inside the mound, alluded to the mysterious sounds of the instruments played by the Muses. According to Francesco de Vieri, a commentator of the period, Pratolino's Parnassus symbolized "men whose lives were dedicated to the pursuit of virtue in the service of the Muses." Pegasus personified their "will to do good" and its wings recalled "the perfect intelligence of this virtue and the ardent Love towards it."[14]

To this synesthetic mountain celebrated by many visitors (including Michel de Montaigne and John Evelyn), it is necessary to add—still in Pratolino—a second important construction that further enhanced the expressive possibilities of the artificial mountain. It is the monumental statue depicting the Apennine, made from 1579 by Giambologna (Jean de Boulogne). Today, the rocky element (the mountain) and the human element (the Apennines represented as a melancholic old man) seem to merge in this work, giving rise to a hybrid being, half-man, half-mountain, half-artifice, half-nature.

Originally, behind the figure of the 11-meter giant that survived—the gigantic sculpture was endowed, like the Parnassus of Ferrara, with caves—there was an enormous artificial mountain, unfortunately destroyed in the 17th century. Pratolino thus contained several artificial mounds: Parnassus, the giant's body as a simulated mountain, the mountain behind the Apennines and, last but not least, the caves as upside down mountains. The latter, the "inner landscape" of the skillfully staged mountain man, was also very remarkable. They housed sculptures of shepherds with their sheep and dogs, scenes related to metallurgy and work in the mines, but also images of fish.[15] The main cave was decorated with corals and other precious materials. The fountain placed in the center of the space, topped by Thetis, was entirely composed of natural materials (shells, pearls, crystals), all assembled following the rules of the most refined art. Vieri's remark, according to which the amalgamation of water, metals and stones within these caverns referred to the concept of spontaneous generation in and by the Apennine itself, shows how this complex construction was conceived as the staging of philosophical ideas.

With Pratolino's Parnassus and Apennines, the rise and spread of the artificial mountains reached its peak. The mountain of Apollo, the Muses and Pegasus sacralize the supremacy of Poetry. The triumph of the *Sacra Poesia* is not limited to the artistic or literary field; poetry, on the contrary, serves as the true source of *sapientia*—of knowledge in general or philosophical knowledge—skillfully represented by Apollo, the god of divination, of the sun and of Truth. Pirro Ligorio, the architect who had a decisive role in the design of several gardens adorned with artificial mountains, expresses this aim present in the symbol of Parnassus. According to him, these artifacts "signified the

RIGHT   Parnassus Room, Villa Aldobrandini, Frascati, etching, in: Giovanni Battista Falda, *Le fontane di Roma nelle piazze e luoghi pubblici*, vol. II, plate 7, ca 1691

weariness and the happy days of those who are devoted to elevated things, and who lead men to the eternal pleasures of ultimate knowledge, to high and deep meditation, perceiving with the eyes of the mind how magnificent is the First Engine that created the heavens and the earth, from so many different inspirations."[16] The wonders unveiled inside the Apennines (inside the lost mountain with its grottoes) linked the aesthetic object mountain-cave to many important questions of the time. By exposing materials from the bowels of the earth, and by thematizing the new science of metals, the Apennines were part of a contemporary discourse on the origin of mountains,[17] on the circulation of water, on the phenomenon of terrestrial and liquid generation, while questioning the meaning of Nature and the relationship between the latter and the arts in general. The artificial mountain, perceptively crossed by extravagantly arranged springs of water, thus brought together in a single object the major ideas of its time. The opposition between nature and history, order and chaos, vice and virtue, and time and space found a powerful means of expression in this major symbol—carefully built in the heart of this most ambitious garden.

The fortune of Mount Parnassus continued in the 17th century and beyond. Think of the famous Parnassus Fountain of the Villa Aldobrandini, this time not in the garden, but inside a room specially designed for its aquatic

theater. Or a work created intentionally as an overcoming of Pratolino's model, the Parnassus in the garden of Somerset House in London. In the western part of this garden, commissioned by Anne of Denmark, the gigantic Parnassus fountain placed inside an octagonal enclosure (under the influence of Francesco di Giorgio Martini?) formed the centerpiece of the garden. The London artificial mountain was able to benefit from the extraordinary knowledge of Salomon de Caus. This inventor and garden designer, for instance of the Hortus Palatinus of Heidelberg, and master of hydraulics, was familiar with the Italian tradition of majestic faux mountains (foremost the Parnassus in the region of Rome and Tuscany) as well as the ephemeral mounds created by Bernardo Buontalenti for the *intermedi*, the theatrical interludes in Florence. The result of Somerset House, described in a testimony of 1613, must have been very impressive:

> On one side, there is Mount Parnassus: the mountain or sandstone rock, with a mixture of all kinds of mussels, snails and curious plants, all kinds of herbs and wonderful flowers emerge from the rock. The opposite side of the Palace is built like a cavern. Inside the Muses are seated with all kinds of instruments in hand. At the very top is Pegasus, a golden-winged horse. On the mountain are four small niches, each with a naked marble statue. In their hands are cornucopia horns and under their arms are vases from which the water flows into a basin four paces wide all around the mountain. They are meant to represent four rivers. Among them a female figure has a gold inscription on black marble: Tamesis. This is the river on which London is founded and which flows near its garden [...] The water flows up to the top of the rock with a stream as big as an arm and gushes here and there from the mountain. It's a magnificent piece that far exceeds Mount Parnassus of Pratolino, near Florence.[18]

The open-air monument in London combines the elements of both Pratolino mounds into one. The presence of the four British river deities marks the transition from the Greco-Roman and Italian model to an Empire that also intends to establish itself, through this symbol of the Renaissance, as a new Parnassus. The mountain of Somerset House, however, marks a major change in the history of the reinvented Parnassus disseminated in the great European gardens of the 16th and 17th centuries. Salomon de Caus' treatment of the mountain architecture—his most famous work, the Hortus Palatinus, also began with the transformation of an uncultivated hill into a mountain-garden—testifies to a much more formal, even casual approach to this theme, which has meanwhile become a cliché. What matters to the French engineer is no longer the abstract concept of Parnassus. The elements listed in the testimony, the Muses, Pegasus, the rivers, etc. seem indeed out of a decoration catalog. It is no longer a question of linking the new mountains to the Greek or Greco-Roman referent, and to the respective mythical qualities of the mountain of

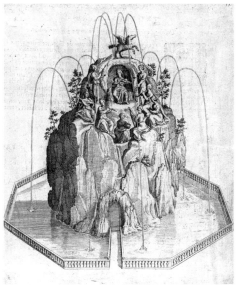

ABOVE Salomon de Caus, *Les raisons des forces mouvantes*, Paris 1624, II, plates 16; 13; 14
NEXT PAGE Plates 10; 11

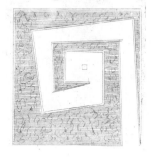

Apollo in the form of a dialogue with the Ancients. The artificial mountains designed by De Caus refer first and foremost to the idea of wild nature. Staging the signifier "mountain" seems therefore to be the epiphenomenon of appreciation for nature among the thinkers of the Reformation in general. The interest in building faux mountains among the French gardener-theorists of the time—almost all of them Protestants—was therefore more theological than mythological. To erect a hyper-visible symbol in the shape of a mountain in the heart of a garden, which for De Caus and his reformed friends also represents the Protestant Church, is no longer simply the expression of an erudite culture, which quotes in a scholarly or ideological way references to Antiquity. Equally essential to this brilliant engineer is the exhibition of his know-how as a builder. The treaty *Les Raisons des forces mouvantes* (Reasons of the Moving Forces) published in 1615, illustrates in the second book under the heading "Problems," a series of artificial mountains which closely resemble the Parnassus of Somerset House. The author explains that he knows and masters to perfection a repertoire of forms ready to be executed on site. As you browse through the magnificent drawings of *Les Raisons des forces mouvantes*, one immediately realizes that the artificial mountain pattern has become an excuse for increasingly extravagant exercises for their own sake. The extraordinary "mountain in the middle of a garden," presented in "Problesme X" is thus detached from any iconographic program. Its primary function is to show the whole garden from a high point of view: "It seems to me that the most beautiful aspect of a garden is to be seen from above." This stone masonry construction was to be fitted with a path leading to the summit and caves inside. By adding that "if you want, you can put a figure, which will sound at sunrise," De Caus indicates the primacy of function, ensured by the technical skills described in the first book, as well as the interchangeability of the semantic elements placed on top of his mountain. For the pragmatic French engineer, the artificial mountain has metamorphosed from a place of representation to a place of experimentation.

1   Ms. Vat. Urb. Lat. 899.

2   "Poichè del tuo trionfo la gran fama/ Di trofei sparsa venne al sacro monte/ Dove immortal si sta chi virtù brama/ Furno le Muse e Febo meco pronte/ A voler tua eccellenza visitare/ Con questa turba e studio congionte/ Questo è Parnaso e il bel fonte, nel quale/ D'ogni dottrina si sazia la mente/ E il petto di ciascun che vi ci sale." (in: Elisabeth Schröter, *Die Ikonographie des Themas Parnass vor Raffael*, Olms, Hildesheim 1977, p. 21, translated by the author)

3   See Louis Cellauro, "Iconographical Aspects of the Renaissance Villa and Garden: Mount Parnassus, Pegasus and the Muses," in: *Studies in the History of Gardens and Designed Landscapes*, vol. 23/1 (March 2003), pp. 42-56.

4   Lactantius Placidus, Scholies of Statius: "umbilicus terrae."

5   "Tangit autem Ennium, qui dicit se vidisse somniando in Parnasso Homerum sibi dicentem, quod eius anima in suo esset corpore." (Schröter, *op. cit.*, note 75)

6   "Iamque Helicon collisque biceps, iamque ungue caballi / fons oriens vatumque virens iam silva videri / incipit et miseris melior fortuna reverti." (Petrarch, *Epist,. Metr.*, 3.1, Ad Johannem de Columna, v. 87-89, translated by the author)

7   "Tunc Elicona nova revirentem stirpe videbis, / Tunc lauros frondere sacras; tunc alta resurgent / Ingenia atque animi dociles, quibus ardor honesti / Pyeridum studii veterem geminabit amorem." (Petrarch, *Africa*, IX, v. 458-461)

8   Giovanni Leoni, *Cristo giardiniere e la corona di simboli. I giardini sulle mura nella Ferrara del XVI secolo*, May 1993, translated by the author.

9   *Ibid.*, translated by the author.

10   I would like to thank the specialist of the subject Ada Segre for this technical and historical information.

11   Strabo, *Geogr.* 9.3.1.

12   "A sinistra di detto Laberinto stava la montagna già nominata fatta a mano, sopra due stanze à volta, che ritenevano la somiglianza di Grotte, l'interiore delle quali era di forma quadrata, non molto grande, lavorata a mosaico, e adorna di Grotteschi e Arabeschi di rilievo gentilmente coloriti, e messi a oro l'altra poi che era la più esteriore era di molto maggiore capacità, e di forma rotonda, ornata anch'essa di vari nicchi, e di pitture parimenti poste a oro [...] E questa Montagna come s'è detto non naturale, ma fatta à mano [...] sopra esse s'ascende per due vie poco meno, che opposte una all'altra, che già erano coperte di pergolati varie sorti di uva squisite, che continuavano anche attorno alla piazza, in cui terminava la parte suprema della stessa Montagna, e che serviva non solamente per porgere commodità di diletto di vista, vagheggiando la città tutta, e il paese vicino, ma anco di Cavaliere à difesa della stessa Città." (Cited in: Costanza Cavicchi, "Il giardino della montagna di sotto o di San Giorgio a Ferrara," in: *Giardini e palazzi rinascimentali di Ferrara: sviluppo urbanistico moderno*, ed. Maria Rosaria di Fabio, Ferrara 1996, pp. 103-119: 104-105, translated by the author).

13   Andrea Marchesi, "Grotte, montagne e fontane estensi: natura artificiata nella Ferrara del Cinquecento," in: *Delizie in villa*, ed. Gianni Venturi, Olschki, Florence 2008, pp. 91-113.

14   "Men whose lives were dedicated to the pursuit of virtue by service to the Muses. Pegasus embodied 'la loro volontà al bene' whose wings recalled 'l'intelligenza perfetta di essa virtù, & l'ardentissimo Amore ad essa'." (Roy Strong, *The Renaissance Gardens in England*, Thames and Hudson, London 1979, p. 91)

15   See Claudia Lazzaro, *The Italian Renaissance Garden,* Yale University Press, New Haven 1990, p. 150.

16   Pirro Ligorio, cited in: E. Blair Mac Dougall, *Fountains, Statues, and Flowers, Studies in Italian Gardens of the 16th and 17th Centuries*, Dumbarton Oaks, Washington DC 1994, pp. 121.

17   See Valerio Faenzi, *Sull'origine delle montagne*, Tarara', Verbania 2006.

18   Strong, *op. cit.*, pp. 90-91.

ABOVE Giovanni Battista Piranesi, *Veduta di Piazza Navona sopra le rovine del Circo Agonale*, 1773

3

A not so ephemeral Mountain
June 8, 1651

One of the masterpieces in art history, admired to this day and commented on incessantly since its solemn inauguration on June 8, 1651, the Roman Fountain of Four Rivers has an enormous rock at its base which serves as a world-mountain. At first glance, the obelisk placed on the superb mound-rock made by Bernini is certainly more attractive to visitors, or the succession of gigantic river sculptures. This composite work presents, in addition to the travertine rock base and the triumphant obelisk, the personification of the four rivers, then considered to be the most important, and a generous basin that surrounds the composition in stone and water. The quadripartite structure identifies the whole as a model of the globe. The four rivers represent, according to the geographical knowledge of the time, the four continents: the Danube for Europe, the Ganges for Asia, the Nile for Africa, and the Rio de la Plata for America.

Installed in the very heart of Rome in the middle of the 17th century, this construction is heavily loaded both in the material (first by the obelisk artfully reassembled and erected on the supporting structure) and in the conceptual or semiotic sense. The history of its construction in the middle of Piazza Navona is, in fact, part of a large-scale communication operation with multiple implications. The first of the messages materialized by the Fountain of Four Rivers relates to the sponsor, Pope Innocent X. For several decades, the Pamphili—the Pope's family originally from Umbria—had begun to occupy and transform this rectangular square, considered an ancient circus of the Emperor Domitian and used since the 15th century as the site of a popular urban market. When Giovanni Pamphili became Innocent X in 1644, almost all of Piazza Navona belonged either to the Pamphili or to their allies, especially the Spaniards. The square, paved in 1485, had two generous fountains designed by Giacomo Della Porta at its ends and a third, more modest one in the middle with an antique basin used as a drinking trough. The political centrality of the Pamphili in Rome—thanks to the Papacy, in principle worldwide, with the center of Piazza Navona acting as a place of power and representation—led Innocent X and his artistic-intellectual entourage to imagine the realization of a work that would act as a superlative attraction in the urban landscape of Rome, which was already well stocked with exceptional objects.

Parallel to the first phase of the project, assigned to the Ticino architect Francesco Borromini, Innocent X began to divert increasing quantities of water

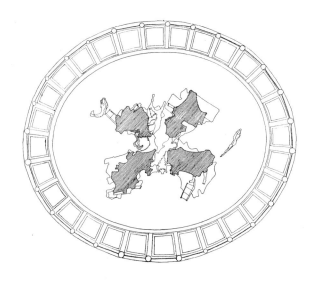

from the Trevi Fountain to Piazza Navona in the spring of 1645. The artistic use of the famous Acqua Vergine, the city's most important source of water—which even survived the sacking of the ancient aqueducts and served as the starting point for the urban planning of modern Rome in the 16th century—is in itself an eloquent gesture. Initially, Borromini worked both on the general concept of the new "monster" fountain and on the realization of the hydraulic system. In April 1647, the Pope visited the Circus of Maxentius where there was a large obelisk in several pieces, which immediately gave him ideas. A year later, in March 1648, he changed project and architect. Seduced by a model of the fountain made by Borromini's great rival, Gianlorenzo Bernini, the Pope officially entrusted the latter with the realization of the new fountain. In August 1649, the obelisk was erected on the rudimentary base of the composition. From 1649 to the summer of 1651, Bernini worked on the project, which was to be inaugurated sumptuously on June 8. The fountain, surprising in its technology, conceptual richness, and daring spatial dynamics, rises to the heavens for the glory of the Pope and his family: it directly looks at or "greets" the Pamphili Palace. The Dove at the top of the obelisk (the only Roman obelisk that is not crowned by a cross) refers to Venus and, through it, to universal love, exactly as the name Pamphili (*pan-phili*). This monument thus linked the new reign of Innocent X to Antiquity, while underlining the pacifying role he intended to play at a very delicate historical moment on the political and religious level (Innocent's predecessor, Pope Barberini Urban VIII had, for his part, waged everything on war). The gesture of personal and clan representation was thus inseparable from the affirmation of the Papacy or

ABOVE/OPPOSITE   The Fountain of Four Rivers, in: Beata di Gaddo, *Le Fontane di Roma*, Vitali e Ghianda, Rome 1964

some other idea of the Papacy as a unifying factor following the terrible Thirty Years' War that had just ended. The erection of a fountain at the center of the world that went so far as to supersede the ancient *miliarium aureum*, the antique center of the world located in the Forum, thus signaled at a delicate moment (the Catholic Church had just lost a large part of Northern Europe) the claim of control over the four parts of the globe and thus over its totality.

Like Mercator's map of 1585-95,[1] which placed a small mountainous island at the center of the globe surrounded by the four continents, the four rivers-continents resting on this mountain-centric island at the center of the world materialized an essential idea of the Counter-Reformation in progress. The obelisk, like an almighty "finger" or "ray," also referred, like the succession of the four rivers, to solar mythology (following the movement of the rivers, the spectator would mentally travel around the world in 24 hours), a situation that implied the thinly veiled identification of Innocent X as a "Sun Pope."

To these personal, political, and religious aspects is added an element, no less important, since the Fountain of Four Rivers also embodies the triumph of Cavaliere Bernini himself.[2] Firstly, let us remember that the ultimate success of his work is inseparable from the existence of several architectural models. If the fountain is, in its own way, encased in a miniature mountain, the series of models illustrating the object to come represented, on closer inspection, the "miniature of a miniature." Legends referring to these objects were already circulating during the artist's lifetime. The best-known story is that Bernini, supported by Prince Ludovisi, is said to have had a small model of the fountain transported in great secrecy to Palazzo Pamphili and that the Pope was seduced by it, suddenly deciding to take the mandate away from Francesco Borromini and entrust it to his rival. By now we know that several other fewer valuable models were circulating in Rome at that time and the legend of a "silver" model probably refers to the practice of making objects of great value

and offering them to high-ranking visitors. For Bernini, the model in question served both as a study, as an instrument of seduction and as a work of applied art. In addition, it made it possible to circulate the image of the future fountain to the public well before it was built on site.

An instructive preliminary drawing, now in Leipzig, shows how Bernini sought a solution to the problem of ensuring a solid base while simultaneously allowing it to take on a cavernous, water-worked form and to carry the weight of the sculptures and the central obelisk. One can detect the starting point marked by the topical shape of the mound, which will eventually take its increasingly light and almost floating form, as well as the intuition of a central crack in the rock suggesting a light ray passing through the set. The panegyric literature of the time and the numerous illustrations referring to it show that the Fountain of Four Rivers was perceived and celebrated from the beginning as a "marvel," worthy of the cabinets of curiosities and other collections of extraordinary objects. The reconstruction of the obelisk, shattered into five pieces, and its elevation alone were already considered a new technological "miracle." However, one also admired the river sculptures and the magnificent details (roses and lilies) engraved in the stone—especially the astonishing dynamic movement suggested by the succession of the four figures. The extreme sophistication of the iconographic program struck the minds of contemporaries curious to decipher this partly explicit, partly mysterious work (it has been fully reconstituted only in the recent studies of Rudolf Preimesberger, Marcello Fagiolo, and Frank Fehrenbach).[3] Moreover, the reception of the fountain must still take into account two fundamental aspects: on one hand, it is a question of following the rhetoric of this great collage, identifying its literary (such as Ovid's *Metamorphoses* and the figure of Phaeton) and artistic sources, without forgetting the non-conceptual or phenomenological access to the work. The Fountain of Four Rivers is, above all, a plastic object that invites the spectator to "walk around" the fountain. However, this "carrousel" quality, amplified by the theatrical setting of the square surrounding it and having created through this fountain a form of fragmented sculpture, has also already been the subject of contemporary commentary.

Enthusiastic admiration and amazement immediately went beyond compulsory reading (its function as a symbol of papal power or as an expression of the *sprezzatura*, the arrogance of the powerful Pamphili), identifying in the

fountain the masterpiece of its author: the eye-
catching sculpture was, in other words, also the
monument to the glory of Bernini himself. Next
to the artist, omnipresent in his work, is another
character. A second author, so to speak, namely the famous Athanasius Kircher. The German
Jesuit, sometimes referred to as the last universal spirit in history, was indeed an extraordinary
jack-of-all-trades. Some forty publications reflect
a wide range of interests that led the author to analyze nearly all the ancient and modern scientific
problems. Endowed with boundless self-esteem,
Kircher was concerned with the transmission of
sound and the magic lantern, bioluminescence
and magnetism, while still believing in the exis-
tence of the unicorn. One of his primary area of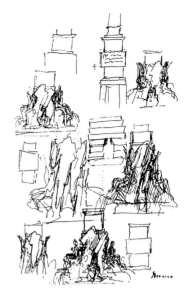
focus was ancient Egypt, which he considered to be the true origin of all civ-
ilization. It is therefore comprehensible that during the discovery of obelisks
in Rome back then, Kircher, who defined himself as the absolute master in
the matter, was approached. Once the project of recovering and reusing the
obelisk was set up, Innocent X ordered his colleague to decipher the text of
the ancient monument. The result was published lavishly in 1650 as a sumptuous volume (*Obeliscus Pamphilius*) when the obelisk was already enthroned
on its pedestal waiting for the other elements of the fountain.

As it analyzed the hieroglyphs before the discovery of the Rosetta Stone,
Kircher's interpretation could only be, evidently, philologically erroneous.
The idea that its message referred to the solar significance of the obelisk was
in any case taken up and integrated into the fountain's design. In the opinion
of Kircher, it is the very deity, which was expressed through the most ancient
signs of ancient Egypt, such as the obelisks. To decipher them, he relied on
a linguistically false, but hermeneutically interesting approach: according
to him, each hieroglyph contained a plurality of meanings that the expert
—rather more a divine than a scholar—had to understand with his intuition.
While the question of the polysemy of the hieroglyph remains open, the large
fountain overflowing with symbols and crowned by the Egyptian monument
is indeed an object literally charged with signifiers. Here, the most different
layers of meaning overlap and intersect, giving rise to a verbal and iconic set
that requires, like the remains of Egypt, to be deciphered. Several elements in
Kircher's works found their way into the Fountain of Four Rivers. Kircher published a book on the hypogeum world (*Mundus subterraneus*, 1665), i.e. on the
relationship between land and water that is a key theme of the mountain-base

ABOVE Gianlorenzo Bernini, *Fountain of Four Rivers*, Leipzig, Museum der Bildenden Künste

of the fountain. He became interested in the mountains of China (*China illustrata*, 1667), including artificial mountains, and he diligently studied Mount Ararat in the context of his research on Noah's Ark (*Arca Noë*, 1675). Working for a sponsor of a prestigious object of absolute visibility, such as the Fountain of Four Rivers, certainly forced Bernini to have intense discussions with the Jesuit father, and he attended like everyone else the famous *wunderkammer* known as the *Kircherianum*. The armadillo at the foot of the Rio de la Plata is not only a local indicator pointing to the American continent, it is a very exact quotation of the animal exhibited in the scientific museum of Kircher at the Collegio Romano and, in a way, the signature of the co-author Kircher.

The fourth and last element in the central fountain of Piazza Navona is the least known and, in our opinion, the most interesting. It is the tradition of ephemeral architecture—Roman but not solely—which precedes and prepares the genesis of the Bernini Fountain. From the 16th to 17th centuries, Rome was the scene of frequent festivities, which required important means to be constructed. Designed by the best artists of the time and realized by a small army of craftsmen, these constructions combining wood, plaster, or papier-mâché, were part of the ornamentation of both secular (entrances, births, weddings) and religious ceremonies. The most significant Roman event of this kind was the *possesso*, the ritual movement that brought the Pope from the Vatican, where

ABOVE Pyrotechnical machine for Pope Innocent X with Noah's Ark on Mount Ararat, Piazza Navona, Rome, private collection, Milan

he had just been enthroned, to the Church of St. John Lateran. Over time, these elaborate public processions took on increasingly sophisticated forms. At strategic places along the route, temporary architectures, artistically designed to attract the attention of the Pope and his cortege, conveyed political messages that were hardly encrypted, in addition to the usual auspicious greetings.

Innocent X's itinerary—in the dual sense of the term, of his ecclesiastical career and his ritual staging—is exemplary in this regard. His *possesso* of November 23, 1644, confronted him with a sequence of communications transmitted with the help of ephemeral architectures. In Piazza Borghese, for example, the French ambassador had a "machine" (this is the specific term used at the time) built to celebrate the triumphant Rome capable of dominating the four continents, a concept that would later be found in the four rivers-continents of the Bernini Fountain. In Piazza Navona, seat of the family palace and the birthplace of Innocent, the procession stopped for the very first time during a *possesso*, while the ritual halt usually took place next door in Piazza Parione.

An imposing mountain-shaped installation occupied the center of the square, displaying Noah's Ark on Mount Ararat. It was a recycled machine, previously used for the coronation of Innocent on October 4 of the same year. The meaning of this ephemeral artefact—an artificial mountain that foreshadowed the subsequent one—was evident: Innocent (his name represented symbolically l'*innocente secolo d'oro*, a new era of innocence and peace) had arrived, like a new Noah after the Deluge and as the Savior of Europe following the terrible Thirty Years' War, after the warrior Pope Urban VIII. Another scenographic machine in front of the French Embassy represented a mountain with a wagon topped by the allegorical figure of France.

The tradition of ephemeral architecture had, of course, distant origins. A date to remember was that of the coronation of Emperor Ferdinand III in 1637 in Rome. On this occasion, Cardinal Maurice of Savoy erected seven allegorical mounds in Piazza Orsini on Monte Giordano. Another mound was built in front of Palazzo Madama. Gianlorenzo Bernini had actively participated in the construction of more than thirty of these architectures cobbled together between 1630 and 1650. In the light of this tradition, the mountain base of the Fountain of Four Rivers appears as the memory and the climax of a practice which, not limited to decorating solemn celebrations and processions, had profoundly transformed the logic of the symbolic occupation of the

ABOVE Luigi Manzini, *Applausi festivi fatti in Roma per l'elezzione di Ferdinado III*, Rome 1637 urban space. A large number of ephemeral constructions prepared Bernini's triumphal project. Marcello Fagiolo identified as possible inspirations, including projects by Leonardo da Vinci (the revolving mountain of Hades), the entrance of Henry II in Rouen in 1550, the entrance of Charles X in Paris in 1571, and a Württemberg wedding in Stuttgart in 1609. He mentions in the same context the ingenious machines of Solomon de Caus, pictorial motifs dating back to the Parnassus of Mantegna, as well as the famous Meta Sudans near the Colosseum.

The base of the Fountain of Four Rivers was borne by the memory of all these mounds. With it, a strategy and way of creating a panegyric work derived from ephemeral architecture became permanent. Although provisional, it is transformed into a permanent structure, the final result, which is the essential aspect, has kept the spirit of ephemeral architecture. This can be seen by observing the lightness of the ensemble, emphasized already in the very first testimonials. While in fact an extremely heavy mass, the construction seems to defy gravity and float on Piazza Navona. It is not surprising that shortly after its inauguration, in 1651, the Pope ordered the flooding of the entire square, presumably following Bernini's advice. The appearance of the fountain-mound emerging from the square's waters, transformed into an antique *naumachia*, must have strengthened the impression of miraculous levitation.

The surprising synthesis achieved by Bernini's work also manifests itself on a semantic level: the fountain manages to balance, albeit in a precarious way, a series of opposing elements. It is both heavy and light, local and global, princely and popular. By revealing "a plea for balance and stability to counter the threat of a disaster"[4] and by affirming the co-presence of opposites, it materializes one of the most important stylistic figures of the time: the oxymoron. The Fountain of Four Rivers is, indeed, an enormous oxymoron: it is half antique, half modern, half remake, half *ex-novo* construction; made of stone and water, wet and dry, stasis and movement, mass and momentum.

The other major feature of the redesigned Piazza Navona landmark is that—directly related to the ephemeral architecture—it demands to be experienced. Drawing its distant origins from the street theater that marked the urban development of Baroque Rome, the fountain requires visitors to revolve around it. The absolute center, petrified and motionless (minus the water gushing out of everywhere) calls for a form of attention imposed by the city at the time on its illustrious or not so illustrious spectators. Furthermore, this construction is grafted onto the countless artificial mountains that have emerged in Italy and elsewhere since the 15th century. Mounds built "solid," but also painted or erected for the duration of a party. The triumph of the Fountain of Four Rivers as an amplified manmade mountain also symbolizes the triumph of the architectural mountain itself. Its integration as part of the

RIGHT *Metae sudantis*, in: Antoine Lafréry, *Speculum Romanae Magnificentiae*, Rome, ca 1593

celebrations in honor of Innocent X is not limited to a stylistic archetype—to a reminder function. Bernini's Fountain quotes the mountain form (mountain-cave, mountain-cavern), while referring to the inherent concept of the term mountain (including Parnassus and Olympus, the mountain of virtue, the theme of ascension). The other rather fundamental aspect is the appearance of form and meaning as such, in other words, how the skillfully assembled object imposes itself onto the attention. The mountain, a quintessentially spectacular form, becomes a sublime mountain-like machine aspiring by its size and context to attract the attention of the whole world. Firstly, the festivals and theatrical scenes, then the increasingly spectacular urban space of the modern city prepared the ground for this epiphany which, as we have seen, favors the mountain shape. Show also means audience member. As a grandiose reminder of the ephemeral mounds of the past, the Fountain of Four Rivers quotes the mode of reception of the latter. The monument designed by Bernini continued in fact to attract people who, trying to stare at it, only managed to turn around in circles. This ultimate centralizing object turns the visitor's head, or better yet, causes him to follow a rotating movement.

Most of the ephemeral structures, arches, rocks, man-made mountains as well as other machines of the time already required a dynamic form of reception: walking around these objects, admiring them from all sides and deciphering their symbols. The Fountain of Four Rivers is, as we have seen, inextricably linked to the solar mythology (Egyptian and universal) and to the diurnal circulation of the sun. Add to this the idea of the island-rock, the privileged mound as the center of the world. This construction is given as an absolute center, a centrality synonymous with the figure of the Pope, his family, the Church and Rome. However, the movement induced by the composition (especially by the succession of river personifications) progresses counterclockwise. One turns and turns again, logically to the left, and not to the right. In a historical period marked by decentration, while this fountain-world expressed efforts to refocus the world, the path suggested by the sculptural ensemble performs a roundabout movement in the "wrong direction." This choice is neither insignificant nor simply an effect of scenography, since it takes place precisely in the midst of a historical moment in which the transition from the geocentric to the heliocentric system is hardly achieved—despite the Catholic Church's resistance, and where the existence of a universe devoid of any center is a topical issue. Giordano Bruno, among others,

said so—at the cost of his life—before 1600. The temporary machine in the most important square of Baroque Rome (Innocent X even wanted to transfer the Roman *curia* to "his" Piazza Navona), which in 1651 became a permanent machine, is very much in the spirit of the center idea. This vertical sign establishes the absolute centrality of the place and its master: Innocent X. However, this is complicated by the fact that one moves around the fountain counterclockwise. A scholarly debate was underway in Europe about the existence of certain shells which, instead of turning in the good direction, to the right, show a rotational movement to the left. The matter related to these natural history samples is teleological; it concerns, in a century marked by Galilei, Descartes, Pascal, and Newton, the problem of the direction and meaning of the universe. As a work of art and a thinking machine, the Fountain of Four Rivers takes part in this debate. The mound-obelisk strongly postulates a center (here, the axis of the world), but it does so arbitrarily. Here and now, Piazza Navona *is* the center, as it best represents the centrality of a form of power that imposes this kind of staging. The set designed by Bernini is, however, a fragile ensemble. Although postulated as "solid," its meaning is exposed to the reading that one makes of it, and therefore to plural interpretations. During the years of Innocent X's Papacy, the discursive system generally provided for compulsory readings. People admired what they *had* to admire, deciphered the allegorical messages, made the links between the Pamphili, Bernini, Kircher, etc. Publications, celebrations, and numerous engravings all exalted the centrality claimed by the absolutist power. Only the popular voice of the *pasquinate*—the witty messages that people put into the mouth of the famous Pasquino—sometimes opposed them, demanding more bread, less expensive constructions, and less taxes to finance them.

The counterclockwise movement and other ironic indicators suggest, however, that Bernini designed for his client an outstanding work of art, without renouncing its "open" (in the sense of Umberto Eco *opera aperta*, the open work of art) and plural quality. The artist gave way to uncertainty, to the concept of "crisis," identified by Frank Fehrenbach, to the tension between equilibrium (center) and imbalance (decentralization). The very idea of conferring to his work a floating aspect is to be related to the logic of a semiotic system based on an overpowering and ultra-solid sign; a sign that is however only a mirage, a lure, an illusion. By erecting a theatrical object within the context of a theatricalized city, with Piazza Navona as the main stage for this show, the artist has infused his fountain, which has been designed for the long term, with something fundamentally unstable.

Therefore, the real danger was for the monument to endure, but for its conceptual quality to deteriorate and, above all, for its political-absolutist message to disappear over time. This form of hermeneutic crisis also happened

LEFT Gianlorenzo Bernini, Giovan Paolo Schor, *Celebration of the newborn Dauphin of France at Piazza di Spagna*, etching by Dominique Barrière, Rome 1662

much faster than expected, with the death of Innocent X in 1655. In 1662, the Fountain of Four Rivers—the grandiose and perennial monument resulting from the tradition of ephemeral festivities—will in turn be symbolically surpassed by new ephemeral constructions.

Ephemeral architecture and the freedom of thought and action is regaining its rights, and it does so by once again resorting to the artificial mountain. Bernini's fountain- mountain-center of the world in Piazza Navona now seemed off-center, as other political forces and other actors were allowing themselves to attract the attention of spectators by using the same object, the faux mountain. The first event dates back to February 1662 and has two protagonists: the newborn Dauphin of France, whose birth was to be celebrated as the representative of a great Catholic nation, and Cardinal Antonio Barberini, nephew of Urban VIII. Barberini, who largely sponsored the festivities, organized the spectacular celebration of the birth of the King's first son in two stages. On February 1st, following a Mass and a *Te Deum* at the Church of the French, a large pyrotechnic machine designed by Giovanni Andrea Carlone was installed in the northern part of Piazza Navona.[5] While the base of the ephemeral work quoted—or better: diverted—the rock of the nearby Fountain of Four Rivers, the statuary's structure took up the number four ("The statues evoke Virtues, the four ages of the world, the four seasons; four tritons blow in their trumpets the glory, supporting a globe surrounded by the palms of victory")[6], thus clearly referring to the quaternary logic conveyed by Bernini as the symbolic cipher of the world divided into four continents. This construction, charged with a series of symbolic elements, ended at its peak with the crown of the French monarchy, which thus claimed the highest position, demonstratively supplanting the Pamphilian dove. The second act, on February 2, 1662, featured a disproportionate amplification of the false mountain theme. The urban space that extended from Via Condotti to Trinità dei Monti had been transformed into a gigantic mountain built by engineers and artists under the guidance of Gianlorenzo Bernini himself. The entire Piazza di Spagna in particular was magically transformed into a huge mountain covered in part by pruned trees and installed to the right measure. The climax of the celebration was the night's enchantment, when fireworks illuminated the whole set admired by the delirious crowd. It is, therefore, particularly interesting that Cardinal Barberini had a lavishly decorated balcony built on the houses facing the artificial mountain, protected by glass and accessible only by the happy few.[7] The show, in a facing arrangement, privatized the public space of the city. The greatness of France, which physically occupied the heart of Rome, transforming it for a day into an allegorical mountain scenery, found its parallel in the scopic device ordered by Barberini to ensure the perfect vision of the show in progress. The Pamphili replaced by Pope Chigi (Alexander VII), it was now the powerful Cardinal Barberini, an ally of France, who controlled visual access to the most expressive symbol in the Eternal City.

Only two weeks later, the same sites—Piazza Navona and Piazza di Spagna—invested to celebrate another birth, that of the Infant of Spain. It was especially so on the third day of the festivities, February 19, since the Spanish ambassador decided to install a grandiose machine in Piazza Navona for the triumphant closing of the festivities. The structure in front of the Palace of Propaganda Fide was, needless to say, a mountain erected, made of rocks and caves and adorned with trees. The upper part, equipped with a solar quadriga, conveyed a meaningful message at the highest point of the mound that once again competed with the Fountain of Four Rivers: it was Spain, just like France two weeks earlier, which now controlled the four continents, with its newborn prince as the new "sun" of the world.

1   See Marcello Fagiolo, "La fontana dei Fiumi alla mostra del Bernini," in: *Roma barocca. I protagonisti, gli spazi urbani, i grandi temi*, De Luca, Rome 2013, fig. 12.

2   See Tomaso Montanari, *La libertà di Bernini. La sovranità dell'artista e le regole del potere*, Einaudi, Turin 2017.

3   Rudolf Preimesberger, "Obeliscus Pamphilius: Beiträge zu Vorgeschichte und Ikonographie des Vierströmebrunnens auf Piazza Navona," in: *Münchner Jahrbuch der Bildenden Künste* 25 (1974), pp. 77-162; Frank Fehrenbach, "Impossible: Bernini in Piazza Navona," in: *Anthropology and Aesthetics* 63/64 (2013), pp. 229-237; Fagiolo, *op. cit.*

4   Fehrenbach, *op. cit.*, p. 236.

5   Martine Boiteux, "Naissances princières: Rome, février 1662," in: *Bulletin du Centre de recherche du château de Versailles* [online].

6   *Ibid.*

7   *Ibid.*

ABOVE   Johann Nieuhof, *Pekkinsa*, etching, 1663

In a chapter of his book *Aberrations*, Jurgis Baltrušaitis juxtaposes in an original way the three styles of French, English, and Chinese gardens. He also makes mention of "artificial rocks and mountains pierced from all sides" which attracted the curiosity of garden lovers in the 18th century. The image of the "rocks made by art in the Pekkinsa village," published in 1735 in *La Galerie du Monde*, shows a strange assemblage of "jagged, twisted forms with numerous excrescences."[1] A few years later, the Jesuit Father Attiret published the description of the Emperor of China's Yve-Ming-Yven gardens. What is surprising about these miniature mountains, which can be up to sixty feet high, is that the rocky Chinese "earthly paradise" appeared as a miniature universe. "Everything that is big in the Emperor's capital is small there."[2] Baltrušaitis compared these "fantasy landscapes" with "artificial mountains, carved in parallel layers, jagged rocks, known to the Sienese since the 14th century, but also to be found in Léonard, Bouts, Herri met de Blès and Patinir."[3]

The existence of this "small world" (Rolf Stein) is, however, originally a distinctly Chinese phenomenon, even if it exceeded with time the confines of China and appeared both in Japan (from the 7th and 8th centuries), as well as in Vietnam. Rolf Stein quotes an exemplary episode:

> During the reign of Dai-hanh Hoang-de of the Earlier Lê Dynasty, in the 6th year, in autumn, at the 7th moon, an artificial mountain was erected, and people rejoiced in contemplating it by boat. That month, during the full moon, was the anniversary of the emperor's birth. A boat was built in the middle of the river and an artificial bamboo mound was installed. It was called "Mountain of the South."[4]

The art of miniaturization that led to the creation of various artifacts has been documented in China since the Tang Dynasty. The precursor of miniature gardens of various sizes is a specific object, the *boshanlu* or *po-chan-lou*, the perfume burner invented during the Han period at the turn of our era.[5] The etymology of the term *boshanlu*, literally translating to "perfume burner of the Bo mountain," remains unknown. There is no mountain of this name in China. The object in question normally contains a lower part with a small column, covered by a conical upper part. This one is composed of a series of triangular vertices. The whole is richly decorated with animals, birds, trees

and sometimes also human forms. The *boshanlu* can be made of bronze or clay. Fine openings between the peaks let the evaporated liquid pass through, suggesting mysterious clouds escaping from the mountain range.

Mountains have always played a crucial role in Chinese thought. Both feared and revered, they gave rise to general and local devotion. Among the most famous mountains, the Taishan has a very simple shape, while Mount Huang, the Yellow Mount, is crowned by seventy-two peaks. The most significant cult was dedicated to the five sacred mountains. These are the Taishan (Sacred East or East Peak) in Shandong, Mount Hua (West) in Shaanxi, Mount Heng (North) in Shanxi, Mount Heng (South) in Hunan and Mount Song (Center) in Henan. These five mountains alone represented all the mountains of the world, as well as the power within them. These mountains were considered to be the main link between the earth and the sky and recognized as the essential source of water.

When a new dynasty was established, the new Emperor had to visit the Five Sacred Mountains and, if possible, climb the Taishan. For at least 2,500 years it has been the site of remarkable pilgrimages. Not far from the summit is a temple that reveals in one of its courtyards the rocky tip of the mountain. This tip, located in an octagonal enclosure, represents the passage from heaven to earth and focuses the energies of the nearby sky according to legend. An essential source for understanding mountain worship is the *Shan hai jing* (The Classic of Mountains and Seas) written around 400 BCE. "As a whole, the book conveys the image of the mountains as a place populated by all kinds of strange animals, where fantastic birds flutter, and strange fish swim or fly with their wings. The mountains were dangerous, inaccessible and filled with powerful mystical energies."[6] It is precisely these fantastic beings that adorn the *boshanlu* and that express perfectly the mixture of fascination and fear of natural phenomena.

These geographically identifiable mountains received an added mountain, this time an imaginary one, Mount Kunlun, in the northwest of central China. Kunlun was regarded as the mythical source of four great rivers (Yellow, Red, Yang, and Black) as well as the seat of legendary deities such as the White Sovereign (*Bai Di*) or the Yellow Sovereign (*Huang Di*). More so than the other five mountains, Kunlun was a crossing point between heaven and earth. The Kunlun, or Mount Sumeru, is imagined as a three-story cosmic mountain, where the Queen Mother of the West lives. A text from the beginning of the Han dynasty, the *Huai nan zi*, says:

> As for Kunlun Mountain, if you ascend two-thirds of the way, you reach the Cold Breath Mountain, where you will not die. And if you ascend another two-thirds of the way, you reach the Hanging Gardens, regain strength, control the wind and rain, and if you ascend another two-thirds of the way, you reach the Upper Heaven and become a deity—indeed, this is the realm of the Great Sovereign (*Tai Di*).[7]

The other element to be considered with regard to the veneration of the mountains is the worship of the Immortals. They inhabit the sacred mountains, and the shamans ensure contact with these spirits. The Han period, the most significant in this context, is characterized artistically by the introduction of the *yunqi*, the cloud spirit, or cloud-breath. It is a curvilinear shape that sometimes takes on the appearance of a cloud and merges with the figures of dragons or birds. The *yunqi* is "a mystical force imbued in a cloud-like form, a form on which the Immortals rode. If seen by people, this was a good omen for the emperor and for society as a whole."[8] At the same time, we find this stylized form, which combines orographic (the mountain, its peaks) and fantastic elements (birds, dragons, human beings), in the precious *yunqi* of the Chinese *boshanlu*.

RIGHT Universal mountain censer (*boshanlu*), Hebei province, Western Han dynasty, 2nd-1st century BCE, cast bronze, Portland Art Museum

The real fortune of the artificial mountain in Asia, however, lies in Japan, and it coincidentally takes place at the same period of the major dissemination of these objects in Europe. During the 12th century, Japan knew of *Shugendō*, a form of religion devoted to Mount Fuji as its main object of worship. The religious syncretism combining Shintoism and Buddhism generally favored the development of a sacred mountain religion, which reached its peak during the Edo period (1615-1867). Already in 1622, the construction of a ritual hut on a *kofun*, an archaic tumulus, is attested without necessarily being an exact imitation of the Fuji.

Fuji-kō, the popular religious movement of Fuji worship, would build up to one hundred Fuji-like mountains in eastern Japan, initiated by Kakugyō Tōbutsu (1541-1646). His follower, and the sixth chief of the Fuji-kō, Jikigyō Miroku 食行身禄 (1671-1733), was responsible for the construction of the sacred mountain replicas in the city. Jikigyō also promoted the idea of a link between rice and the mountains, since water from the mountains fed the rice fields. A small heap of rice thus metonymically represented the mountain, and by eating rice, one nourished one's self with the forces present within the mountain. In 1733, the year following the great famine, Jikigyō fasted for thirty-one days at the famous Eboshi Rock, where he died.[9]

The real promoter of miniature Fuji construction, the *fuji-zuka*, is Takata Tōshirō (1705-1782). This gardener by trade—crucial to the development of the Fuji fashion—climbed the real Fuji more than seventy times and started working on a project of transposed Fuji (*Fuji utsushi*) as early as 1765. In 1779, a six-meter-high mound was erected at Takadanobaba 高田馬場. At its base was, once again, an ancient tumulus (*kofun*) which amounted to building an artificial mountain on top of another one. This double structure, suited Mount Fuji very well—a volcanic mount itself composed of distinct parts (Old Fuji, New Fuji), linked to the different eruption phases of the volcano (the previous one in 1707). Takata used lava recovered from Mount Fuji for the summit of his fake volcano, thus integrating the original material to the copy. In Japanese and more generally Asian thought, there is no substantial difference between the model and its replica, since they are inhabited by the same and universal forces. The new Fuji was not limited to taking the shape of the sacred mountain; it also mentioned the road that went up to the volcano with its emblematic stations, the Eboshi Rock and the altar that crowned it.

In the Suizenji Garden in Kumamoto, created by the Hosokawa family 細川 in the 17th century, the landscape scenes represented the 53 stations of the historic road linking Kyoto to Edo. Furthermore, one of the major attractions of this allusive course was Mount Fuji. Other gardens-walks of the Edo period also functioned on the basis of citations. The creation of ponds, essential in a garden, produced a considerable mass of earth reused in the creation of a landscape created from scratch and which took the form of the reproduction of well-known places. Following the logic of the *shakkeï* (the borrowing of topographies, geographical or mythical recognizable scenes, which is a practice found in the Sino-Japanese garden art), Takata had in any case crafted with his *fuji-zuka* an object of great complexity. Although operating as sacred devices, these Fuji-like devices—at least fifteen were built from 1780 onward—paved the way for a syncretic and unorthodox worship. Other than the "real" Fuji, which could only be climbed by men dressed in white according to a precise ritual, the miniature Fuji worship, scattered in an urban environment, allowed the participation of everyone.

These artificial mountains, which were visited at the same period as the pilgrimage to the natural Fuji, functioned as a mixture between a fair, a theme park and a secular religious center. Three years after the completion of "his" Fuji, in 1782, Takata died and was buried in a final fusion with his favorite object, underneath his work. At that time, the fashion for artificial mountains was also reflected in the shape of *bonsans*, simulated mountain landscapes in a bonsai.

A look back at the great era of *fuji-zuka* is provided by Hiroshige's *One Hundred Views of Edo*. Three xylographs of this series illustrate a simili-Fuji. The first shows a mound erected in Meguro, in 1821, the second the new Fuji, still in Meguro, completed in 1829, the third, finally, the miniature Fuji seen near the Fukagawa Hachiman altar. The sequence seems to tell the story of an amplification that in the end veers towards the banal and the conventional. Hiroshige, to whom sometimes

is attributed a "photographic" style and a representation of codified places under the sign of harmony, appears as a very subtle and ironic observer of Japanese reality. The first engraving puts the mound on the right, at the same height as the Fuji. Both, the original and the copy, are equivalent. The illustration perfectly captures the spirit of Fuji-kō and his omnipresence in

NEXT PAGE   Utagawa Hiroshige, *One hundred views of Edo*, Fukagawa

the region surrounding Edo-Tokyo. The following engraving creates a diagonal between the two, which emphasizes the distance and a certain remoteness. The overall festive impression reflects the transformation of the simili-Fuji excursions into a popular festival. Between the mountain in the distance and the celebrated mound is a hiatus. The final representation shows the artificial mountain as a completely self-sufficient element. The replica has left behind the distant original, it is self-sufficient. The history and the countless references associated with the sacred mountain, the cultural palimpsest built over the centuries, are a thing of the past. Now the Fuji has become a fairground item, a great gadget ready to be multiplied to excess. A lesson to be learned—as we shall see—also in the European context.

1   Jurgis Baltrušaitis, *Aberrations. Quatre essais sur la légendes des formes*, Olivier, Paris 1958, p. 110.

2   *Ibid.*

3   *Ibid.*, p. 123.

4   Rolf A. Stein, *Le monde en petit. Jardins en miniature et habitations dans la pensée religieuse d'Extrême-Orient*, Flammarion, Paris 1987, p. 48.

5   See Yolaine Escande, *Montagnes et eaux: la culture du shanshui*, Hermann, Paris 2005, ch. 2.

6   Kiyohiko Munakata, *Sacred Mountains in Chinese Art,* University of Illinois Press, Urbana/Chicago 1991, p. 7.

7   *Ibid.*, p. 11.

8   *Ibid.*, p. 21.

9   See Melinda Takeuchi, *Making Mountains: Mini-Fujis, Edo Popular Religion and Hiroshige's "One Hundred Famous Views of Edo,"* in: *Impressions* 24 (2002), pp. 24-47.

ABOVE   Jean Tessier, *Vüe du Champ de Mars le jour du 20 Prairial l'an II de la République*, print, 1794

1794: the Mountain of the Supreme Being

The idea of the artificial mountain we are pursuing in this study is intimately linked to certain celebrations. What the various events—weddings, solemn entrances, theatrical performances, etc.—have in common is a type of shared visibility, the spectacular display of a symbol. From the Parnassus-shaped cake to the ephemeral mound exhibited as an exclamation point in the urban space, these powerful signs appeal to a collective and its ability to decipher them far more than to admire them.

The culmination of the French Revolution was also marked by a celebration on June 8, 1794, an event known as the Feast of the Supreme Being. This celebration took place not only in Paris, but in a series of localities throughout France—to the point of virtually bringing together countless people:

> The name of the Supreme Being resounding on the same day, at the same hour, from one end of France to the other! 25 million men assembled at the same time under the vault of heaven, singing hymns and songs of joy to the Lord! What a greater spectacle! What more sublime concert![1]

This event marked the crowning glory of a long succession of revolutionary celebrations that had been in vogue for nearly five years. Like most Renaissance and Baroque festivals, this feast—organized down to the very last details— seemed at the same time spontaneous.

The Feast of the Supreme Being remains as controversial to this day as its central notion, the Supreme Being, or the intentions of its leading ideologue, Maximilien Robespierre. On the other hand, what is generally accepted is the role of this event in the life of Robespierre, who had just been elected four days earlier as head of the Convention and Revolution. It is, indeed, the apotheosis of the Revolution and of its prophet, on June 8, 1794, a culminating point which already hints at an imminent decline. At the Champ-de-Mars, renamed "Place de la Réunion," the most important site and final destination of the ceremony to the glory of the Supreme Being, the mountain served as the main support and primordial symbol. Using the mountain as a major scenic element for the propaganda purposes of the Revolution was not a novelty. The Feast of Reason on November 10, 1793 (the 20th *brumaire* of Year II), moved from Port-Royal to Notre-Dame to mark the occupation of the traditional sacred space by the new symbols in progress and renamed the "Triumph of Reason." A small mound, adorned by a temple with the inscription

"To Philosophy," was erected in the middle of the nave of the old cathedral in the midst of the de-Christianization period. At the foot of the hymn mound, as a republican orchestra sang hymns, the Allegory of Liberty, portrayed by a young girl in ancient Roman attire, sat on a throne crowned by a laurel wreath. By replacing the originally planned statue with a young representative of flesh and blood, the scene on the mound was not only about the substitution of the Virgin Mary for this new "goddess," but also signaled a willingness to combat all forms of idolatry. In other words, it was necessary to insist that the values of the Revolution such as Liberty, Reason, or Truth were embodied allegories and not divinities.

The astonishing fortune of the mountain was certainly linked to the political triumph of the mountaineers, or the political faction called "the Mountain," in 1793. The scale of the construction, its placement in the public space and the very elaborate structure of the mountain of June 8, 1794, however, require a more thorough reading. Firstly, let us not forget the co-author of the event, painter Jacques-Louis David. Grand master of revolutionary celebrations, author of a "citizen" costume (never realized) and of the official proportions of the Flag of France, the artist, who conveniently sat on the almighty Committee of Public Salvation, had from the beginning planned the construction of a generous "amphitheater" in the shape of a mountain. Everything that was supposed to happen at the top of the mound had been decided and fixed by David. Thus he planned a timed scenography with "a first group of drums [that] will be placed behind the Mountain, on the river side"; "the square battalions of teenagers [lined up] into a circle around the Mountain"; "the group of old men and teenagers [placed] on the Mountain on the right"; "the group of young girls and mothers, leading by the hand of children from seven to ten years old [arranged] on the Mountain to the left"; "the National Representation [occupying] the highest part of the Mountain, and the musicians in the middle."

Designed at the beginning of May 1794, barely a month later, on June 8, the festival was successfully carried out. It unfolded like a play in two different scenes. The first act took place in the Tuileries, renamed *le Jardin de la Nation*. Here, the population, cleverly divided into mothers, daughters, teenagers, and the elderly men on the right, and with women on the left, witnessed the symbolic firing of the allegorical figures of Atheism, Selfishness, and other "monsters." In the end, the figure of Wisdom prevailed over these ancient demons, suddenly transforming the ambiguous site (allegorical representation of the values to be fought) into a place of joyful gathering. Everything else took place in a setting dominated by the vegetal element: "All the mothers wore roses, the daughters the most varied flowers, the men the oak logs, the old men the green vine branches."[2] The Convention representatives, on their part, in sky-blue suits, wore large bouquets of ears of corn, flowers, and fruit. This flowered people thus took the appearance of a collective cornucopia. The general atmosphere, which can also be found at the Champ-de-Mars, reminds us of the country festival dear to Jean-Jacques Rousseau.[3] The Supreme Being, difficult if not impossible to imagine, was represented through the "universal religion of Nature." Robespierre underlined it very well in his famous speech of 18 *floréal* II (May 7, 1794): "The true priest of the Supreme Being is Nature; his temple, the universe; his worship, virtue; his feasts, the joy of a great people gathered before his eyes to tighten the two knots of universal brotherhood, and to present him with the homage of sensitive and pure hearts."[4]

The second act of the celebration took place at the Champ-de-Mars, where the procession, meticulously divided into precise sections and typologies, arrived, greeted by young girls who welcomed the representatives of the Convention who had taken their places on the top of the "rock." The music performed a hymn to the Supreme Being, whose chorus was echoed by the audience; 2,400 people on the "mountain" sang the song, followed in part by the enormous mass at the foot of the stage. "The old men and the teenagers placed on the mountain then sang a first stanza to the tune of the Marseillaise, swearing together to lay down their arms only after having annihilated all the enemies of the Republic. [...] Finally, a salvo of artillery, interpreter of the national revenge, resounded in the air, and all the citizens, confounding their

ABOVE *The Population and the Deputies of the Revolution on the Mountain with the Tree of Liberty*, Boulay, Paris, 1794

feelings in a mutual embrace, ended this beautiful day by rising towards the sky this cry of the fatherland: Long live the French Republic!"[5]

It is not surprising that this singular event has been the subject of a pile of interpretations that differ greatly from one another, a mass of words which continues to grow to this day. The range of opinions, more or less solid, goes from the personal project, the expression of Robespierre's strategy or mania, to the collective project carried by the Jacobins, or the collective project of a popular nature. The Feast of the Supreme Being would thus manifest, according to some, the madness or the excessive ambition of the "Pope of a new church," Robespierre. On the contrary, be his political and non-religious instrument, some still see behind the religious symbolism only the new patriotic fervor, or the crowning of revolutionary worship in general. The feast of the "Great Being" is thus characterized both admirable and grotesque, joyful and "cold" at the same time.

It is not our intention to add further considerations to this panorama based on often naive or ideological opinions, convinced as we are that it is fundamentally impossible to separate what is Deism (itself already being a composite phenomenon, marked by Rousseau, Leibniz, etc.), to Robespierre's will to power, to the leadership of David and his brother-in-law, the architect Hubert, or to the revolutionary discourse and machine, extremely organized, ending in the text of the decree of May 7, 1794 with the following formulations: "The French people recognize the existence of the Supreme Being and the immortality of the soul." (I) "Feasts will be instituted to remind the man to the thought of Divinity and dignity of his being." (IV)

PREVIOUS PAGE   Jacques-Simon Chéreau, *View of the Mountain...*, etching, 1794
ABOVE   Ferdinand Bourjot, *Champ de Mars*, print, October 21, 1794

Let us leave, while abandoning the path of great speculations, preferring the signifier erected at the Champ-de-Mars or better, its main component: the mountain. Monique Mosser has shown exhaustively, and on the basis of an extensive archival work, the iconographic implications of the construction of June 8, 1794. The Parisian mountain is linked to the political background of the mountain party, while at the same time functioning as "Nature's hieroglyph." Almost always associated with the circular temple, it fully participates in the emblematic repertoire of the Revolution, in the same way as the fasces, the level, the Liberty tree, the Gallic cockerel or the ouroboros."[6] The second evident reference is, through a "syncretic assimilation," the biblical image of the mountain, especially that of Sinai. "Applied to the feast of the Supreme Being, the mountain becomes the instrument of punishment, while the liberated People dance around the Tree of Liberty, symbol of the early days of the Revolution."[7] A later track identified by Mosser is the "Picturesque Parnassus of Theatres and Gardens." Based especially on the syntagm *temple-rock*, present on the architectural mountain of the Champ-de-Mars, she notes: "The mountain thus appears to be the quintessential natural form, while ideally illustrating the register of the sublime. It therefore merges with a kind of metaphysical image of the absolute."[8] Using the concept of "Masonic impregnation," Mosser analyzes the scene of the festival in light of the iconic language of the lodges:

> The Mountain represented in the revolutionary feasts appears as a "base" symbol in the Masonic tapestries of the 18th century [...] It is most often surmounted by a tree [...] The "up-to-date temple" [...] refers very explicitly to the image of the microcosmic "temple-lodge-workshop," necessarily overhung by the "starry vault."[9]

The kaleidoscope reconstructed by Mosser leaves only one major question unanswered, namely the meaning of the mountain. It can certainly be said that the mountain of the Supreme Being means precisely all the above, that it is both Sinai and Parnassus, the Freemasons' mountain and the Renaissance garden mountain. To better understand the "extraordinary power" of this symbol, the next step involves, in our opinion, moving beyond iconography in favor of a hermeneutic approach. As such, let us consider an object that we have already analyzed here, the Parnassus. It is evident in the context of neo-classicism, of the time and fortune of antiquity, that during the Revolution the Parnassus served as an important model. But which Parnassus is it, and how is the relationship to the sacred mountain of the Antiquity supposed to be thought of? It is obviously not the Parnassus as a form or catalog of themes (Temple, Apollo, Muses, Pegasus, etc.), the Parnassus-container, which we find for instance in Claude Lorrain; it is, if we may express it that way, rather a dynamic Parnassus. In other words, it is the operation Parnassus that now matters, namely the programmatic reconstruction of the antique and distant mountain undertaken from the Renaissance onwards. It is the possibility of combining in a single symbol everything that the era desires as greatness, dream, ideal, and so on, which prevails. Lastly, it is the possibility to build from scratch and to display in an appropriate setting this object that really counts, and not just a mere literary reference. The *tertium comparationis* that the geographic-mythical Parnassus and the Mountain of the Supreme Being have in common only makes sense if its base analogy is fully developed. Because our mountain since 1794 is not *a* Parnassus among others in a historical series—it is the *real* Parnassus since the Paris mountain replaces during this one day everything and everyone in one central symbol.

We agree, of course, on the striking resemblance between the Masonic symbols and this mountain, or others, erected during the Revolution. What seems decisive to us, however, is the demonstrative character of the mountain of the Supreme Being. While Masonic mountains are limited to being represented within a closed circuit, the revolutionary mountain, on the contrary, does everything to show itself. Its model—in the pragmatic sense—is therefore not a particular mountain in the formal or aesthetic sense, but the baroque practice of exhibiting artificial mountains in the politicized context of urban space. Just like the great festive constructions of the Baroque period, which require everyone's attention, and built exactly as they were, with wood and plaster, the DIY architecture of 1794 takes center stage while the Parnassus in the garden have a very different temporality as they are made to last.

Therefore, what is the primary function of the mountain of the Supreme Being? It is about reuniting, gathering, and containing. The Parisian mountain encompasses, concentrates, and it does so in a site that bears its new name of Champ de Réunion. This mountain gathers the Parisian crowd and the whole nation (thanks to its copies) in the provinces. It brings together the different parts of society, merging them through hymn singing and the possibility to stand on or around the mountain. The latter can assume this unifying role as it is regarded as the metonymic sign of Nature itself.

Reuniting also signifies everything that Monique Mosser identified so well, all the iconographic elements mentioned above. Encompassing all of the above references, it gives itself as the visible sign of the Supreme Being or Nature. Applying the "mountain pattern" to the mountain of the Supreme Being, we can easily imagine it as an enormous rock with the Jacobin element at its base, mixed with the Masonic and alchemical element, all of which are associated with biblical and classical references, not to mention the part of the sublime. At the top of the mountain there is, at last, and this is the essence, the Revolution itself. As a force of Nature and an expression of the Supreme Being exposed itself, since it gathers, raises, unites and re-founds the whole of humanity. It is, here and now, on this "cloudless" June 8th, the foundation or base-amphitheater, and the very real majestic rock that carries the new society. On the temporal level, there is a remarkable synonymy between the Revolution and the mountains during this memorable festival. As we had

RIGHT Alexandre-Théodore Brongniart, *Mountain in the Saint-André Cathedral*, Bordeaux, 1793, photo ©RMN-Grand Palais (Musée du Louvre)/Michèle Bellot

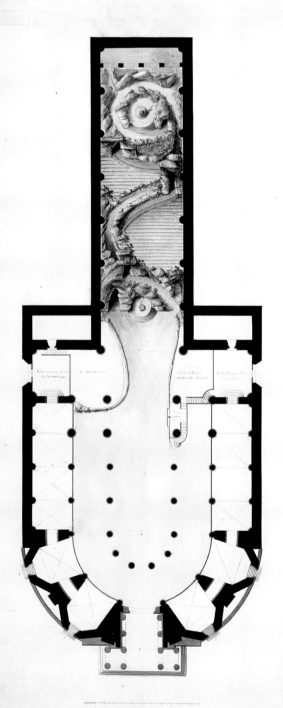

seen, the mountain is occupied and climbed during the ceremony. However, the Revolution was the historical ascent that led to this situation and to this culminating moment. The totalizing form of the mountain—synonymous with Nature and therefore with the Supreme Being—is also manifested in the surprising possibility of encompassing religious discourse. While in 1793, at the time of de-Christianization, an ever-growing division considered dangerous especially by Robespierre, separated religion from the Revolution, henceforth and thanks to this powerful symbol, the revolutionary worship and the religious idea were merging. The mountain built and created by the Revolution, the new universal totality resulting from the battles of recent years, is merged on this historic June 8th with the festive mountain. The tinkered mountain could appear at first glance as a quasi-religious apparatus, an instrument of pseudo-sacralization to better seduce and tame the masses. It results from the Revolution, to the point that one could speak of the "real presence" of the Revolution through and within this mountain.

This sacralization of the mountain as the new absolute symbol of the Revolution—the term understood in its etymological sense as a sign that unites—is also present in a remarkable project by the architect Alexandre-Théodore Brongniart for the Saint-André Cathedral in Bordeaux. Brongniart,

ABOVE *View of the Mountain at the Champ de la Réunion*, Paris, June 8, 1794, etching by Simon and Marchand

involved from the beginning of 1793 in several building sites in Bordeaux (also responsible for the Théâtre Français, which was originally called the Théâtre de la Montagne), had planned a radical intervention in the cathedral which would have literally reversed the logic of the sacred building. The new neo-classical style entrance was to be located in the choir; it would have visually nullified the Christian language of the building and would have led, through what was the core space of the former system, to a new center. Here, a skillfully staged landscape with groves, hedges and a watercourse were to lead, following a serpentine path in picturesque taste, to an artificial mountain occupying the center. The upward movement was to culminate at the top of the mound crowned by the Statue of Liberty. This work, both the construction of a landscape and the deconstruction of the cathedral, used the old sublime of the religious space to transform it into a new sublime, that of a "society of entertainment," a fusion of political and artistic language.

1   *Revue de Paris*, vol. 46 (1837), p. 140.
2   Jules Michelet, quoted in Monique Mosser, "Le temple et la montagne. Généalogie d'un décor de fête révolutionnaire," in: *Revue de l'Art* 83 (1989), pp. 21-35.
3   *Ibid.*
4   Maximilien Robespierre, *Œuvres*, Paris 1967, X, p. 457.
5   "L'Hymne à l'Être suprême," in: *Études révolutionnaires* 17 (1909).
6   Mosser, *op. cit.*, p. 23.
7   *Ibid.*, p. 26.
8   *Ibid.*, p. 29.
9   *Ibid.*, p. 30.

ABOVE Wilhelm Friedrich Schlotterbeck, *Der Stein zu Wörlitz*, aquatint,
based on: Karl Kuntz, *Insel Stein*, 1797

6   *The Wörlitz Volcano*
August 10, 1794

World literature has at least two great novels that can be considered as true "theories" of the garden and its place in the art system: Goethe's *Elective Affinities* and Flaubert's *Bouvard et Pécuchet*. Both books lead to a catastrophe: an existential catastrophe and the failure of a political-philosophical model in the 1809 German novel, as well as an aesthetic and epistemological catastrophe in Flaubert's posthumous work. Although the romantic action of *Elective Affinities* is lost in an aquatic setting (the drowning of a child), it is the metaphor of fire that accompanies and best symbolizes the tragic turn of events. The four friends, who within a post-Arcadian domain tried to carry out a life project alongside a landscape garden project, created an explosive mixture by massively intervening on the local topography and exposing themselves to the dangerous chemistry of human relations. The emotional disorder and disorder within a brutally reshaped nature—with an artificial lake as the symbol and the site of the catastrophe itself—inexorably led to a disastrous end, announced by several disturbing signals. The healing encounter that should have led to the happy end is imagined as such by Edward, the main protagonist: "[...] he asked his friend to warn him of his success at once by an agreed signal, such as a cannon shot, if it was still daylight, or a few rockets if night had already come."[1] After finding Ottilie, his beloved, and before parting from her for a moment, it was again shots that drew attention: "Let us listen! He cried as he rose to his feet in a hurry, for he had just heard a shotgun blast which he mistook for a signal from the Major. It was the explosion of a hunter's gun as he roamed the nearby mountains. Nothing more interrupted the solemn silence of the country, and Edward became impatient and worried." Shortly after the exchange "for the first time, and without constraint, [of] burning kisses" and the violent separation of the two lovers, the drowning occurs, and everything falls into the water (a child, Ottilie, a book, and the illusions of the two lovers). Everything the protagonists and the reader imagined with them turns into a deadly scene: the new Arcadia is indeed stillborn.

The situation in *Bouvard and Pécuchet* seems at first glance much less worrying. The two "fellows" of the homonymous novel devote themselves once their first concerns in agricultural matters are abandoned to the art of gardening. The result of their efforts, initially comic, certainly corresponds to the ironic vein and to the overall strategy of systematic deconstruction of illusions and human stupidity established in the Flaubertian anti-novella. However, dismantling goes further than the destruction of preconceived ideas, including in the garden field, and appears, on closer inspection, to be a real aesthetic debacle:

> It was, in the twilight, something frightening. The rock, like a mountain, occupied the lawn, the tomb was a cube among the spinach, the Venetian bridge a circumflex accent over the beans, and the hut, beyond it, a large black spot, for they had burned its straw roof to make it more poetic. The yews, in the shape of deer or armchairs, followed each other up to the tree struck by lightning, which stretched transversely from the bowery to the arbor, where candied apples hung like stalactites. A sunflower, here and there, was spreading its yellow disc. The Chinese pagoda, painted red, looked like a lighthouse on the vine. The beaks of the peacocks, struck by the sun, reflected back fires, and behind the clearing, cleared of its planks, the flat countryside ended the horizon.[2]

The disorder that reigns in this garden comes from the eclectic mix made possible by the grammar of an artistic production that offered *too* many possibilities. The cataloged garden explodes any unity, thus becoming an involuntary parody of the original intentions.

Both experiments imagined by Goethe and Flaubert are based on a common subtext, namely the syncretic language, which took center stage in the landscape garden from the second half of the 18th century. However, it is possible to indicate a specific site as well as a specific object that served, if not as a model, then at least as a conceptual background to the aforementioned disaster. Indeed, the direct (for Goethe) and indirect (in the case of Flaubert) shadow cast over these failed literary gardens is, paradoxically, that of a garden that has known astonishing success and fame: the garden of Wörlitz in Germany. The object in question, it goes without saying, is a mountain, or better yet, a fake volcano named *Stein* (stone) or *Insel Stein* (stone island). Moreover, its double inauguration took place in the same year, 1794, during which in Paris and all over France other mountains imposed themselves for a brief moment, as we have seen, as symbols of the Supreme Being.

While the Revolution was built and disseminated its neo-Parnassus, a German prince, close to the Enlightenment, was impressing his visitors with his miniature volcano. Its inauguration took place during a highly spectacular power-up. Both in the summer of 1794, to celebrate the visit of King Frederick II of Prussia (a very cumbersome neighbor), and in November of the same year, when Goethe participated in the rehearsal of the event, the mini-volcano of Wörlitz—still 17 meters high—was lit and "exploded" with considerable pyrotechnical means.

The garden of Wörlitz on the banks of the Elbe is the work of Prince Leopold Friedrich Franz of Anhalt-Dessau. The latter, sometimes referred to by his contemporaries simply as "Vater Franz," was like his fellow landscape gardener

in Ermenonville, the Marquis de Girardin; a "damned original," as Napoleon called him. The two shared both an excessive love for the new "fashionable" gardens, studied on site in the United Kingdom, and an enthusiastic veneration for Jean-Jacques Rousseau (the Prince had visited him in Paris on November 16, 1775). Both used enormous means for their garden "madness" and worked for a long time on the composition of their respective works. Wörlitz, the very first picturesque garden on the continent, also paid homage to Ermenonville with the creation of a Rousseau Island modeled on the Isle of Poplars with Rousseau's tomb. The originality of the Prince, who had very early on abandoned the military world he abhorred, also manifested itself in a flippant lifestyle; he had thus decided not to live with his wife, Princess Louise, in the estate's castle, but with the daughter of his gardener Schoch in a house, the future Gothic house (*Gotisches Haus*), less restrictive and closer to his "natural" concerns (gardening, arboriculture, pastoral life). For several decades, in Wörlitz, as in Ermenonville, an ensemble of great complexity was created, to the point of transforming over time the entire small Principality of 700 square km into a *Gartenreich*, a garden kingdom.

The center of the landscaped park was occupied by a lake designed, like a large collage, in several stages from the remains of the Elbe river system. This generous body of water, created especially after the terrible floods of 1770, is both an image of destruction (the permanent danger of floods) and of creation (the victory of reason). The lake is located in the middle of a series of gardens: to the south, the *Schlossgarten* (the castle garden, redesigned in a picturesque style); to the southwest, *Neumarks Garten*, with a nursery and orchards; to the northwest, *Schochs Garten* with, among others, a nymph and a small mound; and in the eastern part the *Neue Anlagen*, or new constructions. All these gardens are dotted with follies. In addition to allegories, emblems and inscriptions of all kinds, there were pavilions, pergolas, urns, a labyrinth and a wide variety of benches. The seventeen or so bridges made of wood, stone, and even steel, told the universal story of bridges from the primitive trunks to the iron bridge (*Eiserne Brücke*), the miniature replica of the first steel bridge that had just been completed at Coalbrookdale, Scotland. The richness of the ensemble—the great connoisseur of gardens at the time, the Prince de Ligne asserted that it took "three days to see everything" in Wörlitz—appears even more important if we consider the mixture of scholarly and conceptual elements referring to the key idea of Reason with follies that simply wanted to move people. The model of most of these objects came from Italy or England. During his Grand Tour of almost two years (1765-1767), the Prince visited the picturesque and sublime highlights on the Peninsula, and his four trips to the United Kingdom allowed him to closely study the most remarkable garden creations of his time. While the Rousseau Island alluded to the Isle of Poplars of Ermenonville and the Chinese Bridge to that of the Kew Gardens, the Temple of Venus referred to the Temple of the Sibyl of Tivoli, and the Temple of Flora imitated a model from Spoleto. The Gothic House, the off-center focus of the Prince's daily life, quoted in its southern part the Gothic Revival set up by Horace Walpole at Strawberry Hill and in the northern part another travel memory, the Madonna dell'Orto in Venice. Some plants also had the function of marking their place of origin. The plane trees (*Populus nigra italica*) forming sumptuous alleys came from Italy, while at the same time functioning as emblems of *Aufklärung*, Illuminism. The agaves and the small forest of fig trees, at the foot of the volcano, were reminiscent of the Bay of Naples, but also of Sicily, and so forth.

If in this off-center domain-state the lake served as the center, the island in the middle was already at that time the focal point of a heterogeneous totality. The volcano island alone is a hybrid object, a collage. It consists of a simulated volcano, a villa, and a Greek amphitheater inspired by that of Taormina, in Sicily. The official itinerary required to approach this spectacular landmark by the waterway, by boat, in order to discover little by little the scene offered to the imagination by the strange mass "that draws all our attention to it. With an attentive gaze and alert senses we continue our navigation to get closer and closer and feel its fantasy effect on our imagination growing ever stronger."[3]

Long before perceiving the layout of the ensemble, one had to follow a tortuous inner journey that alternated horrible effects (the Prince de Ligne speaks of the caves, catacombs and caverns inside the volcano as "scenes of horror," of "a darkness, and frightening stairs"[4]) with the brightness of the saving light ("sudden brightness," "magic glow"). The alternation between the Night Cabinet and the Day Cabinet reinforced this dual effect. The initiatory

journey was characterized by doubt and topographical ignorance: "We walked for an hour in this volcano, without knowing where, how, and why it is one. We only saw the smoky top of the crater which looks like a half chimney and half pyramid."[5] The itinerary through this "land of magic" oscillated between the feeling of the sublime and the pseudo-scientific explanation:

> We climb, not fearlessly, on big stones. We arrive at a basin, which surrounds the first hearth of the volcano, where, when we want to make it play, we make a big fire, so that the smoke comes out through small pipes: and then while still climbing, we see the place of the antique which, mixed with sulfur, coal, and the spirit of wine, becomes by falling all around the crater, a kind of lava.[6]

This near-physical experience of a volcano, through its inner discovery that anticipates the reading of the outside, clearly has several functions. It emphasizes the primacy of sensations over reason and offers well before the explanatory glance and the global narration (linked to the discourse of vulcanology in vogue)—an adventure in the name of the sublime. Furthermore, it allows a descent into the secrets of the volcano that can be interpreted both as a descent into the mysteries of the earth and as a simili-scientific explanation. This sophisticated construction is once again an amalgam of quotations and allusions. The pseudo-Vesuvius is evidently reminiscent of the real volcano that the Prince had "studied" as part of his Grand Tour (he climbed it on February 28, 1766); the Villa stuck against the volcano until forming with it a strange mixture between art and nature, a kind of architectural oxymoron, is of course a reinterpretation of the famous Villa Emma, the residence of William and Emma Hamilton in Naples. Sir Hamilton was the most famous vulcanologist of the time. The British ambassador who spent most of his life studying the volcano of Campania, climbed it well over fifty-eight times[7]; the fig trees, the agave trees and the shape suggested at the edge of the small lake were to recall the gulf of Naples, and so on.

Even in its "extinct" form, this volcano was a spectacular and highly polysemic object. Being confronted with a constructed and functional mountain,
and not just a symbolic volcano machine, it is also to be understood in a hermeneutic sense: this considerable artifact is the result of several strata (the
most diverse ideas being sedimented in it); it is filled with different blocks of
meaning that may explode at any time. Let us try to identify the main strata of this
astonishing construction. The Wörlitz volcano is first of all the representation of
Vesuvius in miniature. The elements of scenography mentioned (Mediterranean
vegetation, coastline) were intended to underline the local, authentic quality of
the transposition. This transfer, carried out in the heart of the domain, trans-
lates an image (it is a cliché, but also the experience of those who had a first-
hand knowledge of Vesuvius) into a miniaturized reality. The pseudo-Vesuvius
is also the symbol of the picturesque garden in general which constantly trans-
lates known images (the topoi of Claude Lorrain: the temple of the Sybil, the
Roman bridges, etc.) into the reality of specific landscapes carefully composed
by gardeners and landscapers. The volcano is at the same time the symbolic
expression of an experience: its author who has been *there*, in Campania, and
who would like to remind it in this composition that could be deemed *Et in
Campania ego*. His volcano is the materialization of his travel adventures, it is a
disproportionate travel souvenir, and the "world" created from scratch in Wörlitz
is also a huge *Reisegarten* (Goethe), or a travel garden. However, the experience

---

in question is also that of William Hamilton and his colleagues, a collective practice, which culminates in the sometimes-exaggerated interest of the time in volcanic phenomena. The mini volcano extends this interest, inscribes it on the ground, and even sacralizes it. Another essential aspect of the experience in play must not be forgotten: the sublime. Even when the volcano was at a standstill, the journey through its internal structure provided thrills that can only be explained by the aesthetics of the incomparably great nature. The unknown object, dark and illegible, terrorized, to give way to a luminous pleasure and a sense of cosmic fullness. This

sublime, however, is not at all the result of a natural object: it is the architecture and the scenography, the technology of representation that are at the source of this mixed feeling. Is the natural sublime that fascinated the 18th century already obsolete in the age of engineers who are now able to build better then Nature itself? Or is it rather a pseudo-sublime, a gigantic simulacrum?

Our volcano is also a mountain cave object in line with the tradition that begins with the Parnassus of the Renaissance. A direct line leads from mounds of the 15th and 16th centuries, through Baroque artifacts related to festivals or theater, to this mountain. While the new Parnassus of the Renaissance was intended as the seat of a newfound fullness, as a reincarnation of what had gone before, and the architectured mountains were erected as all-powerful symbols that demanded a form of collective recognition, this volcano does not embody the distant original: it just copies it, it plays with the volcano form, it illustrates it, without being in any way a volcano or a topographical element of Campania. It rather resembles the countless machine volcanoes, of which Françoise Lavocat has traced the history. According to her, "in the first half of the 17th century, the machine volcano became a privileged device and the motif for large-scale performances, dedicated to the depiction of natural harmony under the pacifying yoke of the prince."[8] Intimately linked to the celebration of the solar monarchy, these volcanoes marked both the "apotheosis and destitution of the enchantment."[9] Lavocat quotes numerous examples of these volcanoes, a kind of magic box filled with firecrackers and fireworks, almost always linked to wedding celebrations. This "barely reshaped volcanic scenery, for half a century, can be found on all the great stages of Northern Italy."[10] The self-poetic quality of these ephemeral constructions, namely "the temptation of baroque theater to call itself an artifice,"[11] is still palpable in the spectacular volcano of Wörlitz. In the 18th century, this "eruptive sublime" became a regular feature of celebrations, especially in Rome. In this context, Kevin Salatino recalled the feast of "Chinea" which, during the festivities of 1727, 1738, 1750, 1756 and 1767, each time called for Vesuvius or Etna, or both.[12]

To these evident components must be added other layers, which are also present in the Wörlitz volcano. Four of these conceptual blocks are mentioned here, without any claim of exhaustivity. The volcano that was climbed from the inside and which brought from darkness to light, is primarily an image of the *Aufklärung*, i.e. of the Enlightenment itself. Now, as we know, the whole of this large, landscaped park and the small principality imagined by the Prince was intended to be a programmatic project. The inscriptions in the park, the control over nature, the Prince's practice as a gentleman farmer, the interest in science and new discoveries (one of the pavilions contained the archives of the navigator Georg Forster), his acquaintances (Rousseau), the area designed as an educational program—everything fits into the overall context of an era that tried, even after the Terror, to reform society and promote the common good. This vein, which partly intersects with elements related to Freemasonry (even if the Prince was rather critical of it), is in partial contradiction with another, no less important one: the erotic vein. Vater Franz, the author of the reshaped domain, which also contained a famous phallic floral installation and not to mention the countless symbols of Venus, did admit that sexuality, particularly his own one, contradicted the path of Reason. In addition, the Garden Labyrinth pointed out the dangers of the senses, while the nearby Elysium advocated Platonic renunciation. And what about the volcano? Did it not indicate that, despite all the efforts of Reason, sometimes history (including the personal history of the Prince) kept moving forward only through eruptions and explosions rather than following the path of virtue? In any case, a recent study has sought to identify in Wörlitz a truly erotic circuit that fits only with difficulty in the general illuminist economy.[13]

More worrisome, however, is the following. The Wörlitz volcano project is taking place at a special moment in the history of science. 1780 is generally regarded as the culmination of an issue that runs through the 17th and all of the 18th centuries, namely the debate between Neptunism and Volcanism. This dispute concerns not only the origin of the mountains—all rocky matter comes from the sea, claimed the Neptunians or Geognostics, while their opponents, the Plutonians or Vulcanians associated it with fire—but generally the increasingly tense relationship between the new scientific approach and theology. Although the followers of the marine explanation were, in general, conservatives (they tried not to cut bridges with a theology still marked by the idea of the Flood), it is rather them and not the liberal Plutonians who provided the basis of modern geology. In the years 1770-1780, particularly

in Germany, the main question related to this debate was mainly about the origin of basalt. The *Basaltstreit*, basalt quarrel, opposed the representatives of the Neptunian position, who favored the idea of order and orderly evolution, to the followers of the "revolutionary" model, who associated the emergence of new forms with the volcanic "chaos." Gradually the Plutonian position imposed itself, at least as far as basalt is concerned: Nicolas Desmerest in France and Johann C. W. Voigt, a geologist from Weimar (a few kilometers from Dessau), in charge of the geological map of the region, advanced strong arguments for the Volcanic theory. Alexander von Humboldt was also convinced of this, in 1790, and in 1805, during one of the frequent eruptions of Vesuvius, Humboldt and Leopold von Buch brought the scientific proof of the origin of this mineral. Goethe himself, extremely interested in the issue, tried to elaborate in a writing of 1779/1780 (*Vergleichsvorschläge*) a middle position.

The Wörlitz volcano has a brick structure at its base, while being entirely covered on the outside by basalt slabs. By exposing this material, it exhibited a particularly "hot" matter that occupied the contemporary scientifical discourse. However, this position, already interesting in itself, does not explain everything at stake. What really mattered, and what is apparent in the allusion to the basalt quarrel, was indeed a teleological problem. The question behind the scientific squabble, however important it may be, was the problem of the

meaning of the universe in general. Was the universe ruled by some higher order, and the Neptunians were right? Was there a regularity in the world, an orderly evolution? Or were the Plutonians right by advocating the birth of order out of chaos? Another problem is intertwined with it, making things even more complicated: was it necessary, on a historical level, to follow the logic of an evolutionary progress that led, for example, enlightened princes like Leopold to privilege Reason, or did history evolve rather by a series of great violent "eruptions" like the one that had just occurred in France?

Read in the light of all these layers the Wörlitz volcano truly contains everything, namely the aspirations, ideas, projects and great intellectual inquiries of its time. The volcano, and by extension the lake, the estate, the state of Anhalt-Dessau, appear as the world, a volcanic world that can constantly regenerate itself. Everything finds its place in this pseudo-natural construction: scientific, religious, mystical, philosophical, masonic, erotic elements, and so on. Like the garden state that surrounds it, the Wörlitz volcano is a pedagogical place that provides its visitors with "supreme" rock-solid knowledge. Using the picturesque and sublime language typical of the time, it also privileges a form of existential experience: to discover the volcano at the center of the garden lead potentially to strong effects and various associations of ideas in the mind of the visitor. The mountain, the ultimate sublime object, is the ideal receptacle for such a totalizing symbol.

This powerful and well-constructed sign meant to contain everything is, however, not really original[14], and most of all, it does not hold because it is

ABOVE *View of Vesuvius before the Eruption of 1767*, colored print, in: William Hamilton, *Campi Phlegraei*, Naples 1776, The Getty Research Institute

too full. It is overloaded and borders on illegibility and even ridicule. This powerful sign is, in other words, a totality that has already exploded. Monique Mosser rightly emphasized the syncretic character of the ensemble ("an amphitheater with gladiator cells, the caves of Misenum, a temple of the night and a temple of the day, a columbarium, the ruins of a *palestra* and the reduction of the Villa Angelica"[15]), a quality of which the author, Prince Leopold Franz, was also fully aware:

> "It's a failure," he confided to the village priest during a walk. It became something quite different from what I wanted. Too many things, too many different things in such a small space; it needed more space... Just think of Winckelmann: Hadrian in Tivoli collected and imitated the masterpieces of art and nature he had seen on his travels through the provinces of the Empire, but he had space. One must not take the liberty of wanting to counterfeit nature in its most monumental and eminent manifestations, in its rocks, its precipices, its valleys, and its volcanoes. In this case we always show things in a very diminished way.[16]

The mountain-grotto, already conceptually endangered in the large collage of the Mountain of the Supreme Being in Paris, marks in Wörlitz the end of a series, which began in the Renaissance (see chapter 2). Here, the syncretic construction becomes senseless, as senseless as the domain which contains it, and which no longer manages to provide a fully satisfactory synthesis of the components that it exhibits. The explosion of the volcano is thus also the spectacle of its dissolution (like the explosion of the house at the end of Antonioni's *Zabriskie Point*), or what amounts to the same, of the atomization of its parts. Such an amalgam—and the author of *Elective Affinities* has clearly understood this—is not only obsolete on the political-social level (the time is no more that of excessive individual projects, of bucolical daydreaming and aristocratic retreats), it is above all problematic on the aesthetic level. The explosion in the figurative sense (the volcano as a simulacrum) creates the disorder which, around the crater, the center transformed into an anti-center, becomes the new landscape. It is the disorder of a world—the picturesque garden is its life-size playground and laboratory—that contains *too many* different things to be brought together in a coherent whole, no matter how extensive it may be. What remains then is only a field of ruins (the ruin itself is only the ruin of its ambitions) and a context where everything appears only to put on a show. The strange mixture inside and in the immediate proximity of this "rock" that has lost its solidity already clearly announces the syncretic crisis of the European garden art in the post-revolutionary period. The faux mountain at the heart of the Wörlitz experiment expresses perfectly the crisis of the impossible totality of the garden (which is now based on a too rich repertoire, on the possibility to reassemble all the cultural references of the world in one spot, very well illustrated in Gabriel Thouin's *Plans raisonnés de toutes les espèces de jardins*) and the crisis of a political model that cannot be anymore, after the revolutionary eruptions of the 18th century and the reaction to it, the society of everyone and everything.

The analysis of our volcano and its surroundings indicates, behind the personal failure suggested by Prince Leopold Franz, a much broader and worrying phenomenon. This hyper-ambitious object is, in other words, the symbolic materialization of the "dialectic of the Enlightenment." Too much knowledge, more and more (modern) knowledge, including encyclopedic access to knowledge (this will become one of Bouvard and Pécuchet's lines of thought), can no longer lead to supreme unity. The new totality, ever changing and deprived of cohesion, the collage, the assembly, and even the most audacious construction, although driven by Reason, can only explode. This Faustian situation, so characteristic of the time, leads to the violent dissolution of the totalizing sign, the supreme symbol which, in principle, was supposed to guarantee ultimate unity. Instead of the full, complete and solid sign, here is an object that does not reflect the path of a victorious synthesis, but, on the contrary, its impossibility. The ambiguity of the project, both the acme and the failure of an absolute ambition (it is indeed the pinnacle of the landscape garden), also results in the replacement of the rational and the illuminist model (the lost totality) by a model that will only be accessible

ABOVE   Remigio Canta Gallina, *Intermedio quinto di Vulcano*, Wedding Celebrations for Cosimo de Medici, Florence, 1608, MoMA, New York

through sentiment (the felt totality). While the volcano fails on the rational level, it has already announced itself as a spectacular object of a new kind, full of "mystery," a romantic object, which speaks directly to the "heart" of "sensitive souls."

1   Johann Wolfgang Goethe, *Die Wahlverwandtschaften*, II, ch. XIII.
2   Gustave Flaubert, *Bouvard et Pécuchet*, Conard, Paris 1910, p. 61, translated by the author.
3   August Rode, *Beschreibung des Fürstlichen Anhalt- Dessauischen Landhauses und Englischen Gartens zu Wörlitz*, Tänzer, Dessau 1798, pp. 231-232, translated by the author.
4   Charles Joseph de Ligne, *Œuvres*, Complexes, Bruxelles 2006, vol. 3, p. 217.
5   *Ibid.*, p. 218.
6   *Ibid.*
7   Monique Mosser, "Allégorie naturelle et poétique tellurique dans les jardins pittoresques de l'Europe des Lumières et de l'Illuminisme," in: *Les éléments et les métamorphoses de la Nature*, Annales du Centre Ledoux, vol. IV, William Blake & co, Paris 2004, pp. 379-406: 394.
8   Françoise Lavocat, "Un 'nuovo, e meraviglioso et horribile soggetto'. Le volcan dans l'opéra-ballet et le théâtre à machines," in: *L'imaginaire du volcan*, ed.: Marie-Françoise Bosquet, Presses Universitaires de Rennes, Rennes 2005, p. 2.
9   *Ibid.*, p. 3.
10 *Ibid.*, p. 4.
11 *Ibid.*, p. 11.
12 Kevin Salatino, *Art incendiaire. La représentation des feux d'artifice en Europe au début des Temps modernes*, Macula, Paris 2014, p. 79.
13 Michael Niedermeier, *Angestammte Landschaften, mystische Einweihungsräume und arkadische Liebesgärten. Gartenkunst der Goethezeit*, VDG, Kromsdorf 2017.
14 Mosser quite rightly quotes a remark of Chambers, which more than anticipates the Wörlitz volcano: "The illusion will be maintained by a volcano artistically built in imitation of Vesuvius and which will throw flames by means of charcoal." (*Ibid.*, p. 397)
15 *Ibid.*, p. 396.
16 *Ibid.* "Vater Franz" confuses space and time; it is time, and not space, that makes things impossible.

7 *The Pyramids of Branitz*

On July 20, 1973 the American artist Robert Smithson, accompanied by his photographer, flew over the artificial lake of Tewokas, Texas. Smithson was working on what would become his latest installation, *Amarillo Ramp*. On that fateful day the small plane crashed at the project site. Nowadays, the lake has completely disappeared because of the drought and his anti-monumental ramp is exposed to erosion. The fusional union with his own work, set in a man-manipulated desert, is reminiscent of another, much older fusional act. In 1871, the heart of one of the most famous garden designers and theoreticians of the time, Prince Herrmann von Pückler-Muskau, was rather solemnly incorporated into a large mound. The pyramid-shaped mountain, built in 1854 by the Prince in the middle of an artificial lake, covered with grass and containing the remains of the German aristocrat, is located in Branitz near Cottbus, Brandenburg. Here is the contemporary description of the strange funeral ceremony:

> There was the heavy, yellow oak coffin in the middle of the room overflowing with royal luxury, the velvet green wallpaper with white and red lights, which came from outside through the curtains covering the polished windows, and all of this created a magical reflection above the candles at the top of the cenotaph. The illustrious dead carried nothing with him except his last bed with its massive silver ornaments and palm branches, crowns, and plant arabesques. [...] The church having finished its service around the coffin, the procession set off to the muffled sound of the drums of the military band. [...] The black and white feathers of the deceased's helmet flew from the coffin on which the knightly sword with its noble sheath was laid. In the copper urn adorned with flowers carried by an officer behind the coffin was enclosed the heart of the deceased according to his last wishes. His last wish had been respected to the letter: the doctors in charge of the delicate mission had carried out the dissection and chemical decomposition of his entrails and the funeral procession was not heading towards a cemetery, but towards the three gigantic pyramids to the west of the castle. The northernmost was the final destination of the procession. It rises in the middle of a lake. It is there that the Prince foresaw his last resting place. A wooden bridge erected temporarily brought us beyond the lake, to the base of the pyramid. [...] Here we are standing in front of the passage dug in the pyramid which led to a space without embellishments and covered with simple wooden planks, it had a volume of about eight cubic meters.[1]

The person who bid farewell by ordering: "Level the way to the Tumulus!" was indeed an extremely eccentric figure. Born in a small principality which he would personally take care of until its annexation by Prussia, the young man and future great traveler first undertook a Grand Tour of four years. Returning to Muskau and succeeding his father, he wanted to reform his small kingdom of 41 villages and 11,000 inhabitants, based on a project that favored the aesthetic approach. Like Leopold from Dessau-Anhalt in Wörlitz, Pückler had decided to turn the "desert" of Muskau into a huge garden. Although his grandfather Herrmann von Callenberg had already established a park on both banks of the Neisse, the historical vicissitudes of the years 1810-1815, which the young Pückler spent in France, Switzerland and Italy, had almost completely disfigured the site. As early as 1815, Pückler began work on the development of his estate. He alternated periods during which he was active on site with numerous trips that allowed him to become familiar with the most important gardens of the time and the projects of the most important landscape architects. In parallel with his fieldwork, the Prince cultivated his theoretical knowledge by studying the writings of Hirschfeld, Repton and Sckell, among others. His approach, in Muskau and later in Branitz, owes much to the Reptonian method, an intellectual debt that he admits in his 1834 work, *Hints on Landscape Gardening*.

The practitioner and theorist Pückler favored the establishment of large visual openings (*Sichtachsen*) and the arrangement of skillfully composed land-scapes according to the pictorial succession of the three planes (foreground, middle plane, background). He also made a name for himself in moving very large trees, an arduous technological task for which he even invented a very impressive *tree-machine*. The Muskau park, which exemplified his garden phi-losophy, also had a generous ground adorned with rose bushes and equipped with specific furniture. The fact that the *Hints on Landscape Gardening* illustrate the ideal and not the real situation in Muskau is related to the main difficulty encountered by the Prince-Gardener, namely the costs of the venture. His large-scale projects had very quickly confronted him with an unsustainable financial situation. His reaction—perfectly in keeping with the character—was to travel even more (leaving the 600-hectare estate to his wife Lucie) and, exposed to a dramatic situation, to the decision to divorce his wife (without really separating) in order to marry an heiress who could cover the costs of his "green" passion.

In 1845, however, Pückler had to face the evidence of his project's fail-ure and sell Muskau, which, as he said, had become his "chimera." This date also coincides with the start of his second major landscaping project, in the Branitz estate, which was much smaller than Muskau. The failure of his ju-venile utopia altered his overall vision of the garden (while Muskau was ac-cessible to everyone, visitor's access to Branitz was strictly filtered), without changing his stylistic orientations. In his second domain, too, the eccentric prince gradually transformed an almost deserted, wasteland garden into an

extraordinary, landscaped park. It has been calculated that between 1846 and 1870 almost 11 km of trails were created, not to mention the planting of a million trees and the displacement of 100,000 m³ of material. Pückler, who was always in search of unity and totality—the garden had to appear as "a well-ordered ensemble"—adorned the estate with follies of all kinds. Most of the pieces scattered in the garden were directly linked to the author's person: the statues of Venus and the pergolas were reminiscent of the beloved and partly imitated Italy; the monument to Lord Byron's dog was an allusion to Byron's garden and Pückler's admiration for it; the bust of his father-in-law and the small temple for a singer also underlined personal links. In his private paradise, Pückler built a kind of museum of memory piece by piece, that is of his individual memories translated into the garden. The contemporaries had already noticed that visiting Branitz was quite similar to a theatrical show. After getting your entrance ticket, one methodically followed the route planned by the host, discovering one act after the other, scene after scene. The opportunity to meet the owner-director, now self-transformed into a legendary character, was the culmination of a visit that increasingly assumed the character of an initiatory experience.

The place of interest for us is in the western part of the Branitz inner park (100 ha, the outer park covers 600 ha). The west, chosen by Pückler because of its connection with the setting sun and with the concept of transcendence, forms a sort of vast private necropolis, marked by three mounds: the Lake Pyramid, erected from 1855-56, the Terrestrial Pyramid, initiated in 1862 and, finally, the *Hermannsberg*, the construction of which began in 1868. The existence of these three faux mountains is linked to the creation of two artificial lakes: the Pyramid Lake (*Pyramidensee*) and the Serpentine Lake (*Schlangensee*). It is important to point out that, regardless of the symbolic connotation and cultural and personal allusions, these three objects out of context—Branitz is

located in an entirely flat environment—are the result of an exemplary constructive gesture for picturesque gardens. Indeed, most of the irregular gardens designed in the 18th and 19th centuries had to have one or more small lakes with undulating banks. By keeping and accumulating the extracted material and giving it a pyramidal shape, the topography of the redeveloped park emphasized the relationship between empty (hollow) and full (mountain), as well as the enormous energy expenditure necessary to its realization. In addition to the obvious link between land and water, it is the dialectic of destruction (digging into the earth, creating a mountain in negative) and construction (elevation, creation from a privileged point of view) that appears as the striking character of the site. What is "told" or memorized by the topography, is perfectly suited to the mystic-romantic image that the Prince intended to suggest through his "Totenhain,"[2] his grove of death.

The major element of the Branitz mortuary complex is therefore the pyramid. The English-style garden is from the beginning marked by the presence of pyramids. They can be found in the two main gardens of Rousham and Stowe, but also, in Germany, in Gotha, Machern, Garzau, Dessau, Hohenheim... Since the 18th century, the pyramids have been a real cliché in the great European parks. One of them is still visible in the Parc Monceau, a monument designed by Philippe d'Orléans and built between 1773 and 1778. Endowed with a space which one had to cross, the hollow of the pyramid meant to initiate the visitors to the rites of Isis reinterpreted in the light of the Masonic rituals then in vogue. At Maupertuis, in 1781, the Marquis de Montesquiou also erected a pyramid, this time in memory of Admiral Coligny, a martyr of the Protestant cause. Built as a false ruin, the pyramid of Maupertuis immediately showed the imprint of time, which accentuated its picturesque appeal.

Pyramid fashion was a huge success in Germany, where such constructions are countless. However, most of them did not imitate the Egyptian model, but rather the pyramid of Cestius in Rome, a monument that was very well known by the Grand Tour travelers.[3] Its location in the non-Catholic cemetery of Rome and the decadent aspect conveyed by the engravings of Piranesi, had added to the original meaning of the pyramid as a monument to the origin of culture itself, the Romantic idea of death. In the *Isle of Death* with its pyramid of Wilhelmsbad near Hanau, Hesse, built in 1784, Egypt, ancient Rome, the Isle of Poplars of Ermenonville and the taste of the time for elegiac feelings merged together. Another important pyramid, also inspired by that of Cestius, was located on the Wilhelmshöhe of Kassel. Erected in 1775, next to a "tomb of Virgil," it is testimony to the rampant popularity of this symbol, which is also present in Kassel on the *Isle of Roses*, with its pyramidal tomb built for the dog of William II, Erdmann.

In addition to the fashion trend, the simple imitation and the masonic element, a third aspect must be added: the sublime. Whether it is already with Athanasius Kircher, in the 17th century, and in a mure subtle way, with Piranesi in the following century; or, in an even more palpable way, with Boullée who projected extraordinary pyramids-cenotaphs, what imposes itself each time is the disproportion between the out of measure dimension of the pyramid and the relativity of the finite human adventure. The pyramid is, at least in the 18th century, an exemplary form of the sublime, since it evokes, in addition to the immediate impression of disproportion between the greatness of the object and the smallness of human existence, an air of mystery supported by what contemporaries imagined as typically Egyptian.[4] With the pyramid, interpreted as an expression of the first civilization, the imagination

ABOVE Athanasius Kircher, *Sphinx mystagoga...*, Amsterdam 1676

could project itself into a vast and unlimited space-time. As a symbol intimately linked to burial, the pyramid also opened up a future space-time, that of life after death, which is also infinitely more extensive than life down here. It is precisely this atmosphere tinged with the sublime of death—an atmosphere à la Mozart—that the episode with Pückler's entry into his pyramid illustrates so well: an Egyptian and Roman sublime, neo-classical and romantic, and above all a perfectly staged theatrical sublime.

To better understand the last representation of the Prince—"my ultimate piece," as he would call it—, it is important to have a more precise look at his personality and his work. We know that Pückler willingly defined himself as a "butterfly," that he boasted about his adventures of all kinds, his encounters with the great personalities of his time, his knowledge of the world. We also know about the politically incorrect episodes during his trip to Egypt, when he "bought" four young slaves, later getting rid of three of them and bringing his favorite with him to Germany. What seems rather relevant to us, however, is to propose a different reading of his last act, a reading that is both less and more personal.

Let us note first of all that the problem encountered by the Prince in Muskau belongs to his entire era. Ulf Jacob noticed that Pückler acted, from the beginning to the end of his first garden project in Muskau, in the manner of a feudal potentate.[5] The attempt to reform his property on the basis of Enlightenment principles failed not only because of economic and political constraints, but also because of the irreconcilable contradictions between the views of a prince (and the control exercised over his kingdom, however small) and his subjects. The failure of Muskau's project, i.e. the impossible application of St. Simonism to the local reality, led Pückler to increasingly bitter, even cynical positions. Following the collapse of his first large-scale experiment, he multiplied his travels (he became increasingly a "butterfly") and began his second work, Branitz. As he developed his *ferme ornée*, he metamorphosed not only into a gardener or a landscape architect, but into an artist. In other words, he chose the identity of the landscape gardener-artist as a life-form, since it was the only one that allowed him to transform almost all of his life into a work of art. Since he represents the rather exceptional case where the owner of a large garden is also its creator, the garden became indeed inseparable from his person, it *became* totally Prince Pückler (or he became the garden). Other than in Muskau, in Branitz he did no longer care for people, being only interested in "nature." His actions were now

purely aesthetic, and encompassed his own person. The form and life of the garden are not separable from the author who expressed himself completely in it. This also explains why everything in this garden was in Pückler's image. Branitz was consequently visited in the manner of a theatrical performance and the meeting with the director crowned the experience of the garden.

Pückler made it clear to everyone that the only interesting form of life was the one he had chosen, a life that revolved entirely around the garden. Projecting, planting, moving, measuring, comparing on the ground, but also talking about the garden, describing it, being its recognized specialist—all of this was part of a single life project. In the last century, aristocrats and landowners had already created extraordinary gardens (Stowe, Stourhead, Rousham, Ermenonville, the Retz Desert), but they had done so using gardeners, landscape architects, architects and advisers of all kinds. Kent, Bridgeman, Brown, and Repton had designed extraordinary gardens, yet they did it for their clients. One can, of course, cite the exceptions marked by the poet-gardener Shenstone, but *The Leasowes* is a tiny estate compared to Branitz while Pope, who created Strawberry Hill, which lacked the true professional know-how that characterized Pückler.

The owner of Branitz had succeeded in transforming his garden into a truly existential place. Certainly, English garden theorists influenced by empiricism

had already spoken of the need to allow oneself to be immersed in a garden and to find oneself transfigured as a result of the personal experience of a well-composed garden. While these authors spoke of the effects of punctual visits and the discovery of specific gardens, the fact that his own life and his garden became inseparable transformed the Prince's daily existence into something exceptional. The radical quality of this second part of Pückler's life was not the result of his real extravagance, but rather of the fusion of all aspects of his life in the phenomenon of the garden. Since the Prince lived this totality in a permanent way, nothing was insignificant or, what amounts to the same, everything became meaningful and representative. With Pückler the garden was a work of art, but so was his life, not to mention the writing that kept its traces. When looking for a literary parallel for this extreme form of practice, it is not the protagonist of the *Domain of Arnheim* of Poe that comes to mind (in his case, it is the new fantasy landscape that counts, and much less its author), but Monsieur de Risach, the aristocrat-hermit of Stifter's *Late Season*. The connection with Stifter and his escapist, even reactionary vision of the world, naturally raises the question of the "price" of the experiment set up by Pückler. Did he not achieve his second masterpiece only by "cheating," by going through a pseudo-marriage that ensured the expenses of his new madness? And (leaving aside for a moment the aesthetic aspect, which is certainly preponderant) what about the political and social implications of such an extreme work? Did it not lead the Prince to a form of staging and a cult of his own personality that made him a squared lord, a super-powerful post feudal potentate in a society already marked by industrialization?

By creating his garden in this way and advocating this form of life as a supreme freedom, it was clear that Pückler had to conclude his life *in* his garden. The terminal fusion in or with his pyramid is his last utterance, his final (garden and landscape) speech act. What makes it original is the reinterpretation of the *topos* of the pyramid in the garden. While most of the other pyramids were made of stone, the Branitz pyramid is an "Erdpyramide," an earthen pyramid. The body of the "Erdbändiger," the landscape gardener who has mastered the earth, ends up in an earthen construction, a "living" object, so to speak. While its shape recalls eternity, its material refers to a more complex aspect. The pyramid ages and it is exposed to time; eternity, thus consists in the unceasing transformation of everything that exists, an idea suggested by the oriental culture of the Prince. The pyramid is also the omnipresent reminder of his personal knowledge of Egypt. The mystery of his personality and everything he discovered there, merges with the mystery of ancient Egypt. This powerful symbol can be analyzed in the garden (and by visiting other monuments), but it will always keep—just like this work—something enigmatic and secret. At his death, Pückler "entered" his pyramid, which now and for the time to come welcomes his heart. As the deceased, he does the same thing he did during his lifetime: he became absolutely inseparable from his garden. The presence of his remains in this object that attracts all the attention recalls by its sublime greatness the greatness of the person who built it. Just like an Ouroboros, the circle closes and takes the "Green Prince" with it.

1   "Da stand der schwere gelbe Eichenschrein in der Mitte des von königlichem Luxus strotzenden Gemachs, dessen grüne Sammettapeten mit den weißen und rothen Lichtern, welche von außen her durch die Vorhänge der geschliffenen Scheiben fielen, und den zu Häupten des Sarges brennenden Kerzen einen magischen Reflex schufen. [...] Die Geistlichkeit hatte inzwischen ihre Amtshandlungen am Sarge verrichtet und unter dem Wirbel der gedämpften Trommeln des vorausziehenden Militärs setzte sich der Zug in Bewegung. [...] Von dem Sarge wehten die schwarzen und weißen Federn des Helms des Verblichenen, sein erprobter ritterlicher Degen mit dem edlen Gefäß lag auf dem Sarge. In die umflorte kupferne Urne, welche ein Officier hinter dem Sarge nachtrug, war das Herz des Todten eingeschlossen, wie er es gewollt. Man hatte seinen letzten Willen in allen Punkten erfüllt: die damit betrauten Aerzte hatten die Section und chemische Zersetzung seiner Eingeweide bewirkt, und der Leichenzug bewegte sich nicht einem Kirchhof entgegen, vielmehr auf die drei riesigen Pyramiden im Westen des Schlosses zu. Die nördlichste von ihnen war das Ziel des Zuges. Sie erhebt sich aus der Mitte eines Sees. In ihr wollte der Fürst den letzten Schlaf thun. Eine provisorisch gezimmerte Brücke führte uns über den See hinüber an ihren Fuß. Wir standen vor dem in denselben hineingetriebenen Stollen einem schmucklosen mit einfachen Bohlen ausgeschalten Raum von etwa acht Kubikfuß Größe." (Paul Wesenfeld, "Prinz Hermann von Pückler-Muskau," in: *Die Gartenlaube* (1871), 10 et 11, pp. 164-167, 180-183, translated by the author)
2   Jan Pieper, "Semilassos letzter Weltgang. Der Totenhain des Fürsten Pückler-Muskau in Branitz," in: *Daidalos* 8 (1990), pp. 60-79.
3   The cork models of the pyramid of Cestius were popular souvenirs among travelers; see Annette Dorgerloh, Michael Niedermeier, "Pyramiden im frühen Landschaftsgarten," in: *Pegasus. Berliner Beiträge zum Nachleben der Antike*, 7 (2005).
4   See Aleida Assmann, Jan Assmann, *Hieroglyphen. Stationen einer anderen abendländischen Grammatologie*, Fink, Munich 2004.
5   Ulf Jacob, *Hermann Fürst von Pückler-Muskau – ein Künstlerleben*, in: *Parkomanie. Die Gartenlandschaften des Fürsten Pückler in Muskau, Babelsberg und Branitz*, Munich 2016, pp. 23-39.

291 — PARIS. Le Parc des Buttes-Chaumont. ND I

ABOVE Buttes-Chaumont, postcard, 1916

A Mountain in the Heart of Paris

> The thought of our time is to make us love nature. Romanticism has rid us of the fetishes that did not allow us to see it, understand it, and love it for itself. What we want to teach our children today is that grace is in the tree and not in the hamadryad that once inhabited it; is that water is as beautiful on the rock as it is in marble; is that the hideous rock itself has its physiognomy, its color, its cherished plant whose windings make a marvelous hanging; is that the rocks do not need symmetry and shell coating: it is only a matter of imitating, with a loving skill of the true, their natural dispositions and their monumental, comfortable or whimsical poses. Later on, if our children see how true nature proceeds, they will taste it, only better, and they will remember the rocky outcrops of Longchamps, Monceaux, and the Buttes-Chaumont as we remember with pleasure and affection the little slender plant that we have grown on our window, and which we see, powerful and grandiose, blossoming in its homeland.[1]

This dithyrambic text by George Sand salutes the great achievements of the Second Empire and—first and foremost—the creation of the famous Buttes-Chaumont Park. At its inauguration on April 1, 1867, in conjunction with the opening of the Universal Exhibition, the city of Paris unveiled a surprising work to the world. In just three years, one of the unhealthiest places in the capital had been transformed into a gigantic example of "nature in the city." With a popular vocation, but linked to the program of a new residential neighborhood, the reinvented Buttes-Chaumont advocated loud and clear the synthesis between advanced technology and nature rediscovered, or better yet, nature brilliantly staged. Although the Buttes provided well-proportioned lanes, carefully prepared for elegant strolling—with stairs and bridges for easy traffic—they reflected the idea of wilderness *via* the aesthetics of the picturesque and the sublime.

The highest point of the complex, located on a perimeter marked by the fluidity of the ellipse (representing a vast island within the Parisian urban landscape), consisted of an artificial mountain of great complexity. An important and lasting mountain built by mankind that, for the first time, was no longer the expression of the prince's will, but a non-exclusive artifact intended for a popular reception. In the middle of an artificial lake of 1.5 ha, the island-mountain proudly soared towards the sky, allowing a new and unusual view of Paris. The Belvedere at the top of the architectural mountain adorned with a kiosk-replica of the temple of the Sibylle of Tivoli, gave this site a pastoral look (made however possible by a hyper-technological intervention). As if by a magic trick,

this new park had erased a previous reality that had represented for several centuries a cursed place in the Parisian imagination.

The "buttes," integrated into the city of Paris only in 1860 and which belonged to the shady districts of Belleville and La Villette, formed mounds of clay and marl resistant to any vegetation. Gypsum and millstone extraction sites, they contributed to the edification of Paris, while passing for a peripheral and particularly sinister place. It is here, in this steep and uncultivated desert, that horse carcasses and debris of all kinds were disposed of; interestingly, these places had been used since the 14th century as gallows of royal justice. It is here again that the debris of revolutionary destruction ended after 1789. In the 1860s, at the beginning of the construction of the future park, these "bald" clay mountains (*Chau-mont*) were considered particularly horrible and feared for their malodorous emanations.

In 1867, when Napoleon III and his wife inaugurated the park, they discovered a completely remodeled topography where the telluric element (cliff, rock, mountain, cave) appeared mixed with the aquatic (stream, waterfall, lake) and vegetal elements. The buttes, generously tarmacked, offered a variety of walks, one more surprising than the other. One was struck to find in this urban Eden a huge 19-meter-high cave decorated with stalactites, or a stream emerging from nowhere. There were both a masonry bridge and a dizzying suspended footbridge. These visual stimuli often also had a geographical meaning: thus the cliffs at the base of the redesigned mounds evoked the famous cliffs of Étretat in Normandy, and foremost, the gate of Aval. A different section of the park, titled "Little Switzerland," was meant to bring back picturesque Swiss memories, while the Vosges or the Himalayas were present by their vegetation. The presence of flora from all over the world on the site close to the Universal Exhibition also underlined the spirit of openness of this park, which also offered belvederes and new viewpoints of Paris. The success of the Buttes-Chaumont was in any case immediate. It was impossible not to

ABOVE   The Buttes-Chaumont before the park project, author unknown

admire the passage from the desert on the fringe of the stinking and chaotic medieval city to the flowered paradise corresponding to the image of a modern city which, in these same years, also "flowered" in the Parc Monceau, or within the two urban forests of Vincennes and Boulogne. The formidable marketing operation so representative of the spirit of the Second Empire and the Haussmannization of Paris had indeed replaced the wasteland by a sophisticated construction that offered interesting nooks and crannies to explore everywhere. The itinerary, very easy to follow, displayed nature in miniature close to actual reality; it aroused sublime shivers and invited the discovery of picturesque landscapes, all offered to the whole population in a green setting guaranteeing both healthiness and access to fresh air. The realization of this "tour de force" (Alphand) was possible thanks to the investment of enormous financial means and manpower. The titanic project required more than 1,000 workers, roughly 100 horses, a system of wagons on 40km of rails, two steam engines, and plenty of dynamite to blow up some of the existing rocks.

This project and the respective worksite have benefited, not as a secondary aspect, from the attention and active collaboration of the best professionals in the field. Moreover, we have already noted that the construction of the artificial structures analyzed in our study almost always called upon the expertise of the eminent specialists of the time. Building artificial mountains is a matter of extreme complexity. The Buttes-Chaumont is no exception to this rule. Leading this project (leaving aside the wishes of Napoleon III and Baron Haussmann) was first Adolphe Alphand, the engineer of bridges and roadways who directed all the work of the city of Paris under Haussmann. Alphand was appointed director of public roads and promenades in 1867, the year of the exhibition and opening of the Buttes-Chaumont, and redesigned the Trocadéro and the Champ-de-Mars. Pierre Barillet-Deschamps, the chief gardener of the city of Paris, was also involved in the adventure of the Buttes

ABOVE   The Buttes-Chaumont, n.d., photo: Charles Marville

from the beginning. He worked on the project with Édouard André, Alphand's right-hand man and his successor at the head of the Paris gardens. Essential to this small group was the engineer Pierre Darcel and the architect Gabriel Davioud, chief architect of the Promenades of Paris, as well as the rock contractor Eugène Combaz. The latter had already worked with Alphand in the Bois de Boulogne, where he realized the waterfall and the artificial rocks, and also at Longchamp, where he also built a waterfall. His major contribution to the Buttes-Chaumont consists in the great cave. Combaz developed a method for making stalactites on site by coating the iron rods previously fixed on the cave wall with fresh cement.

The park is therefore the result and showcase of at least three different entities. First of all, it is the expression of the Haussmann system, i.e., an operation that is both economic and political in its control over urban space. With regard to this aspect, the hygienic approach goes hand in hand with a functional view: the newly developed city was healthier, but it also facilitated movement through a set of arteries that allowed in extreme cases to control crowds. The fact that one could circulate so easily and efficiently inside the Buttes-Chaumont Park and that it was crossed by an interior alley, precisely designed for traffic, which is added to the beltway, is a perfect expression of this desire for spatial control. The second force that literally materializes at the Buttes is the construction technology of the time, embodied by the figure of the engineer.

Alphand and his team represent a form of expertise that really made the difference. Like Central Park in New York, Les Buttes-Chaumont is one of the world's leading examples of landscape architecture in the strict sense of the term, i.e. interdisciplinary work driven by the mastery of modern techniques and recognized experts. Problems of identification and nomenclature referring to the Buttes-Chaumont (Is it a park? A garden? A square?) reflect this new situation very well. Antoine Picon has shown the extent to which this pseudo-natural space actually exalts unparalleled technological performance.[2] Picon rightly calls it "a kind of cement and concrete museum" in the open air. Through this park, presented to the world at the 1867 World's Fair, the engineers provided vivid proof of their know-how and the domestication of nature by man.

The "debauch of cement" and the tinkered rocky forms refer, however, to a third skill at the origin of the Buttes: that of the rock workers or *rocailleurs*. The contractor Eugène Combaz, who also worked on the construction of the aquarium for the exhibition at the Trocadéro, belongs to this third category, whose history has been traced by Michel Racine:

> Buttes-Chaumont represents "the best demonstration of the French teams' mastery of cement in the landscape. The new material allows the construction of a retaining wall 2 meters thick by 50 meters long and 15 meters high to retain the clay under the old boulevard Veracruz, a 2-hectare lake with a cemented

ABOVE The Buttes-Chaumont, postcard, n.d.

bottom, the consolidation of the existing cliffs and the rock remodeling. The island and the needle that accompanies it are doubled in height, 'without an attentive observer being able to see the difference between the two parts,' notes Edouard André. The cement also allows the realization of a staircase of one hundred and seventy-three steps along with two streams, the dressing of the cave with giant stalactites, the realization of waterfalls, and innumerable rustic fences in fake wood. Thanks to it once again, the rocks were reconstructed and terrain became accentuated to better suggest certain geographical landscapes: the cliffs of Étretat by the lake, the Alps in the valleys and on the heights."[3]

The Buttes-Chaumont, which began to dominate the urban landscape of Paris in 1867, functioned therefore as a multiple signifier. They represent Napoleon III and Baron Haussmann, but also the figure of the engineer and the *rocailleur*, as well as the spirit of the bourgeois-entrepreneur who plans, builds, moves and amazes the public by creating increasingly extraordinary objects.

An initial flaw in the system and a major contradiction is, however, announced if one considers that this symbolic artifact of technology gives itself as a romantic object. Here, avant-garde technology did not create an object with a technological aspect; it preferred to present an image of nature, or better, of fictitious nature with a fake waterfall, a fake cave, a fake stream, and a faux mountain. Picon is right to say that at the Buttes-Chaumont cement and concrete can be found almost everywhere, but it is only the trained eye of the specialist that can detect them. For everyone else, this representation and tinkering with nature merges with nature itself.

Let us come back to the central part of the complex, to the island within the island, to the mountain placed in the middle of the lake. This telluric mountain-cliff-rock-cave complex, which also serves as a support for the "alpine" landscape, is the highest and most over-determined sign of the Buttes-Chaumont. In the dramaturgy of the promenade, it becomes the culminating moment: this is where all the paths lead, this is where the climax of the promenade is. Arriving at the top and discovering the surrounding area from the kiosk is not a trivial experience. To contemplate the city from this elevated vantage point is—we are long before the Eiffel Tower, another "gift" given to Paris at a

---

World's Fair—a privilege offered to everyone. The reinvented Buttes are, in other words, also a great platform for everyone to enjoy a panoramic view of the capital.

This mountainous part of the park recalls specific geographical landscapes, such as the cliffs of Étretat and the Swiss alpine landscape. These two referents, Étretat and the Swiss Alps, were chosen and staged thanks to their sublime and picturesque qualities. The Normandy cliffs seen from a low vantage point form a majestic wall that strikes the visitor. Their whiteness transforms them into an epiphanic spectacle, giving them the quality of pure aesthetic appearance. Furthermore, at the time of the Buttes-Chaumont project, the admiration for the cliffs of Étretat had reached its peak: everyone was flocking to Normandy to admire them, including writers and painters. By imitating them, the

E. V. 563 PARIS (XIX¹) – Buttes Chaumont – Une Cascade

Parisian artifact thus quotes a quintessential auratic object, or perhaps it does not quote the object, but rather its aura. The same applies to the alpine landscape, which is also part of the picturesque canon clichés.

Here is a work which, while being composed of a series of artificial elements (fake cliff, fake rocks, fake mountain, fake cave, fake waterfall, fake stream) is at the same time almost a mountain and almost a cave. The relationship between the original (Étretat, Swiss Alps, Tivoli) and the copy is not that of identity, but that of resemblance. The Buttes-Chaumont, seen from the lake, look like the Normandy cliffs. And as time goes by, they increasingly resemble nature. The result of this operation of urban "embellishment" is thus necessarily ambiguous: one discovers something that is much more than a copy without being in any way an original. The suggested resemblance (a common feature of picturesque 18th-century gardens) represents a completely arbitrary act: the cliffs of Étretat or the ideal landscape with the Temple of the Sybil are quoted here, but other elements could have been drawn from the available repertoire (as early as the 1820s, Gabriel Thouin had listed an extremely rich catalog of such possibilities). Charles Baudelaire, the most lucid witness of the transformation of Paris under Haussmann, understood the logic of this kind of operation. The famous verse from his great poem *Le Cygne*: "Paris changes, alas and everything becomes allegory," perfectly identifies the mechanism at the origin of Haussmannization, since under the direction of engineers and capital, everything seems to have been turned upside down.

ABOVE The Waterfall at the Buttes-Chaumont, postcard, n.d.

From now on nothing remains in its place in Paris. The Buttes-Chaumont, an ironic symbol of this operation now coming to an end, crushed the old mounds, highlighting new allegorical signifiers such as "Étretat," "Tivoli" or "Swiss Alps." The new Buttes-Chaumont mega-sign is therefore just as artificial as the city being born under Haussmann, where everything can be torn down and replaced to make way for something else. It is also in this sense that we can understand the idea expressed by Louis Aragon in *Le paysan de Paris*, which identifies the Buttes-Chaumont Park as "the unconscious of the city." It is precisely by excessively pushing a trend that characterizes an entire era and transforms, during a little less than a decade, the French capital completely.

The Buttes-Chaumont Park is not a small object lost in the countryside of an aristocratic owner like the volcano of Wörlitz. It is a highly visible presence in the "capital of the 19th century" (Benjamin) that takes full advantage of the attention and the brilliance of the World's Fair. One could even argue that it belongs, in terms of its artificial structure and spectacular logic, to the exhibition in its own right. It is, in other words, the eloquent expression of a new historical reality where nothing is ever in its place, where everything moves like merchandise. The Buttes from the Haussmann era are exactly that: a huge product made from scratch using the latest technology of the time. Besides, the speed at which the Buttes were constructed reflects the generalized acceleration that strikes this period, a temporality whose symbol Baudelaire identifies in the "new" Carousel.

However, to make the Buttes last beyond the time of an exhibition is not self-evident since keeping them in this new form as an almost natural object requires considerable means and energy. All observers pointed out the technical problems of maintenance, collapses, falling rocks, etc. However, as soon as time—or rather true nature, the one that attacks and ruins things—starts to work on this object, it inevitably distorts it and risks revealing both the defects and the underground mechanics that ensure the illusion of the ensemble. In order to avoid this calamitous state of affairs, it must be permanently maintained. This constant work must however be concealed since its visibility would suddenly cancel out the aura of the object. The Buttes remain to this day, in the general opinion, the "most natural" park of the French capital thanks to a very heavy maintenance activity. Central Park in New York, another mega-park born out of a huge wasteland poses quite similar problems. The Buttes are therefore not only a simulacrum in an aesthetic (a simulation of nature), but also in an operative sense: it is the hidden work that keeps this sublime and picturesque show alive. The sublime, important to remember, is far from being a "natural" or innocent phenomenon. Hartmut Böhme showed in his essay "Das Steinerne" (the rock-like), that the climax of the sublime in the 18th century coincided with the occupation of the last corners of the earth

TOP RIGHT   Anonymous drawing of the Buttes-Chaumont
BOTTOM RIGHT   Adolphe Alphand, *Les promenades de Paris*, Paris 1867

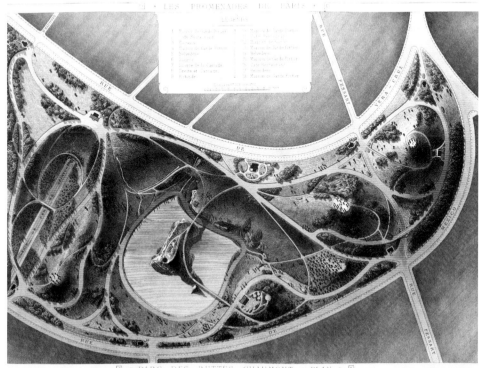

PARC DES BUTTES CHAUMONT · PLAN

by the victorious capitalist society.[4] Once man, and above all the engineer-entrepreneur, controls the totality of nature ready to be exploited and knows all its secrets, he will do what Alphand and his team have accomplished at Les Buttes-Chaumont and elsewhere: he will build an artificial nature from scratch. The combination steep rock/suspension bridge which, seen from a low vantage point, makes you dizzy, is also a replica. It clearly imitates a situation discovered and codified in the 18th century, present both in Caspar Wolf's classical landscapes and in Turner's romantic visions. The naturally sublime, barely invented by John Dennis and his followers from the 1680s and already transformed in the 18th century into a tourist value, is replaced by the sublime assembled by the engineer.

The comparison of the new Buttes-Chaumont with the artificial mountains of the past reveals in any case an essential difference. The Wörlitz volcano was still, in its own way, a volcano, at least once a year at the time of its "explosion"; the Branitz pyramid was a real funerary mountain since it accommodated the remains of its creator; the Renaissance Parnassus were certainly pale copies of the Greek original, but they nevertheless functioned as symbolic places of a palpable cultural revival. But what about the Buttes-Chaumont? The difficulty in finding the right name for it (is it park? a place of entertainment?) immediately identifies it as an unclassifiable object. The Buttes are, in truth, a materialized "Parisian dream," a generous piece of pseudo-nature, a nature more attractive and fascinating than the real one. They function as a vast set inside a stage with an organic form, a fiction that the municipal machine keeps in order so that the show can go on. Thanks to this sustained effort, visitors could discover here, where nature is exhibited like in a museum, a world in miniature. It was a bit of the Vosges, a bit of Switzerland, a bit of Italy, a bit of Normandy, a bit of the Himalayas, it was all the elsewhere at once, within reach. For the visitors, the Buttes contained and absorbed the whole world, similar to the World's Fair.

However, the problem with manufactured products is that they tire after a while as they go out of fashion. This is what also happened with the Buttes, which, once the initial enthusiasm had subsided, would no longer satisfy the bourgeois public. The real estate project originally planned would not see fruition, partly explaining the disinterest of the bourgeoisie, which turned to other objects of desire. Once disappeared from the radar of the happy few and people of taste, the Buttes-Chaumont will found at least one of their original vocations: to function as an oasis of greenery for a neighboring working-class population deprived of fresh air and places of leisure.

1   George Sand, "Les promenades dans Paris. La rêverie à Paris," in: *Paris Guide*, Paris 1876, vol. 2, p. 1202.

2   Antoine Picon, "Nature and engineering: the Buttes-Chaumont park," in: *Romantisme* 4 (2010), pp. 35-49. See also Isabelle Levêque, "The park of Buttes-Chaumont, theater of memory of the engineers of the Second Empire," in: *Jardins de France*, SNHF, oct. 2002.

3   Michel Racine, *Jardins "au naturel": Rocailles, grotesques et art rustique*, Actes Sud, Arles 2009, p. 87.

4   Hartmut Böhme, "Das Steinerne. Anmerkungen zur Theorie des Erhabenen aus dem Blick des Menschenfremdesten," in: *Das Erhabene. Zwischen Grenzerfahrung und Größenwahn*, ed.: Christine Pries, Weinheim 1989, pp. 160-192.

ABOVE Le Château d'Eau, 1900 Paris World's Fair, postcard, n.d.

9   *The Electric Waterfall*

Objects, even when they are massive, tend to move. They move through space and time, and they do so especially if they belong to the same series.[1] Thus the fountains of Rome moved, so to speak, continuously from the 16th century onwards. A hardly excavated ancient basin was used as a base for a new construction, adorned with an obelisk from afar and new masks made for the occasion. Over time, many of these massive elements were transposed from one site to another, as if the aquatic dynamism of the fountains began to touch the substance of these monuments of the modern city.

Another artifact had a similar fate in the 19th century: the artificial waterfall. Waterfalls erected by considerable means and admired by the public cross the history of major exhibitions and, in particular, electrotechnical exhibitions of the time. One of the most important of these electric waterfalls is the one from the Munich exhibition, inaugurated on September 16, 1882. The symbolic representation of nature in the form of a waterfall fountain—the main attraction of the Munich event—was part of an ingenious device that connected the town of Miesbach, 57 km away, to the Ice Palace of the Bavarian capital. The electric current, generated elsewhere thanks to a steam engine, was transported over a distance almost unimaginable at the time of more than 50 km, powering a Dynamo machine at the other end, rotating the 2m high pseudo-cascade. The staging of the 2CV production provided a showcase for the cutting-edge technological advances of the day. The waterfall project, and generally speaking the exhibition, was the work of the visionary engineer Oskar von Miller. He did not intend the event to be a fair for specialists only; on the contrary, he wanted to seduce the general public by exhibiting the extraordinary novelties of the day, such as the telephone or the electric light that illuminated the towers of the two great Munich churches during the exhibition. Technique and art were to transform the whole into a gigantic enchantment, capable of captivating visitors. In any case, Von Miller's efforts for scenography bore fruit, as the enthusiastic testimony of his contemporaries shows:

> At the entrance of the building, the gaze was delighted by the magnificent play of colors that formed the flower and plant bed ordered with a masterful hand. From the top, the bluish light of the arc lamps fell generously, and in many places the reflections of the water jets from the fountain illuminated by headlights shimmered—a spectacle that no one will ever forget.[2]

The 1882 installation, financed by Alphonse de Rothschild, has a major place in the history of electrification, economics, and technology. It aroused almost universal enthusiasm. Von Miller himself noted: "When I gave the signal and the engine started to run, when the centrifugal pump came into action and the waterfall started to rustle, the excitement was so great that you cannot even imagine it today."[3] What is most important in the context of our inquiry is the symbolic significance of the waterfall as a central and vivid part of the exhibition. Integrated within a large rock, surrounded by fir trees, with the spectacle of the water in the middle, the waterfall appeared clearly as a *pars pro toto* of the mountain in general. The fake waterfall within the fake mountain, which Von Miller and his partners were very fond of, was not just an electric machine; it functioned as a device that provided meaning to the technological innovations of this period. Three aspects are particularly interesting in this context: the integration of the topical artificial mountain in the framework of a technological exhibition, the annexation of Nature, and lastly, a scenography with a new form of the sublime.

The 1882 artifact clearly represents both the memory and the overcoming of the past. In the past, ephemeral mountains were built in Europe, as we have seen, with the primary function of transmitting (ideological) messages. While the architectural mountains of the Renaissance and the Baroque period overwhelmed spectators thanks to their powerful scenography, the constructions of the French Revolution used the mountain as part of an ambitious political operation of legitimization. Artificial mountains were therefore always linked to the discourse of power and control, a gesture that the mountain, visible from everywhere and overwhelming in its size, symbolized to perfection. The Munich device, followed by a large number of other examples, sometimes amplified in size, is also ephemeral. It transcends however the idea of the ephemeral, since its very aim was to symbolize duration. Even if von Miller and his collaborators had to struggle with the reliability of the transmission, which in reality only worked for a short time, the important thing was the public demonstration of a system that promised endless electrical happiness. By exhibiting a technological cascade, more artistic than natural, near a chapel equally illuminated by the new electrical lightning, the electro-theatrical scene of the Munich exhibition suggested in a barely veiled way a fundamental substitution. It was the replacement of the old sources of legitimization, apparently religious, by the new source of electricity. Long before the analogy between electricity and divinity expressed by Henry Adams in a famous letter—"this is a new century, and what we used to call electricity is the God of it"[4]—von Miller's installation already put on show the technological source celebrated as the modern-day cornucopia. By associating the rock mountain with the waterfall fountain his scenographic machine amalgamated several lines of tradition from the history of architectural artifacts of the past. The fountain-waterfall that apparently turned on its own represented the image of *another* nature made possible by the miracles of modern technology, a more powerful and self-sufficient nature. As a *nymphaeum* of industrial culture, it suggested a new purity and simplicity, embodied in the field of triumphant engineering. Meanwhile, the rock containing the installation was a symbol of absolute solidity and a palpable materialization of the electrotechnical system.

One can easily add other elements present in the model of the electric waterfall with remnants of a past both used and outdated. Thus the sound and light of the scenography shown in Munich (von Miller underlines the miraculous sound of the waterfall fountain illuminated by the bluish light descending from top to bottom) evidently refers to the luminous enchantment of baroque machines. Similarly, the skillful assembly of the mineral and the liquid is reminiscent of the work and the know-how of the *rocailleurs*, whom we met at work at the Buttes-Chaumont. While artistically-minded engineers were tinkering with pseudo-natural objects such as the Munich waterfall, gardeners and landscapers were fascinated by the possibility of creating artificial waterfalls from scratch in landscaped parks, carefully assembled and brightly lit thanks to the modern technological innovations.[5]

By consulting the documents of another electrical waterfall, that of the electrotechnical exhibition in Frankfurt am Main of 1891, designed under the direction of the same Oskar von Miller, the characteristics of this highly symbolic object become even more evident. Less than ten years after Munich, the new exemplary demonstration now focused on the extraordinary distance of 175km. The distant water source, the Neckar river, fed indirectly the large waterfall at the entrance to the technology fair as well as a thousand lamps. Once more, recent first-rate innovations had overcome all obstacles and presented the result as a true revolution that would change the future of humanity. And here again is the waterfall, augmented and more abstract, a kind of gigantic ready-made, which illustrates the passage from the prehistory of electricity to its proper historical phase. More so than in Munich, Frankfurt's tinkered rock seemed to come out of the catalogs of the landscape architects capable of constructing mineral forms to their own liking. The programmatic presence at the entrance of the Electric Village, however, also drew attention to an essential phenomenon—namely the annexation of nature by mankind. Using the system developed by the engineers, it was now possible to produce energy everywhere, even in remote areas, and consume it elsewhere, in energy-hungry

cities. The line that united the far away source and the finishing point, culminating in the higly visible electric waterfall, marked not only the route from the periphery to the urban environment, but also the one that led to a nature definitely subdued in the name and thanks to the financial possibilities of the modern industrial society. By erecting electric mountains with a waterfall, the players in this "revolution" programmatically announced (probably without being fully aware of it) the complete and definitive occupation of the entirety of nature by humankind.

However, the metonymic quality of the electrotechnical waterfalls of this era goes even one step further, if we consider that the device put in place is not limited to the annexation of distant energy sources. As new manmade mountains and waterfalls, these objects presented themselves as the tangible evidence of the possibility of actually building mountains, waterfalls, as well as nature from end to end. These new demonstrative constructions, exhibited at popular events and visited by millions of people, represent at the same time the definitive triumph of a new type of sublime. Rediscovered and theorized between the end of the 17th and the beginning of the 18th centuries, the sublime was applied for the first time to nature at the same period. The natural sublime that succeeded the rhetorical and theatrical sublime amounted to something incomparably great, which produced, as Burke and Kant explained well, in the mind of the modern subject a mixture of terror and fascination.[6] While the 18th and 19th centuries used the fascination with the sublime promoting the phenomenon in the context of "sublime tours," the second half of the 19th century was already replacing the natural sublime, often downgraded to a cliché, with a new object of desire. It is the majestic works of engineers and architects, i.e. bridges, viaducts, tunnels, and buildings that started to count in this new era. A direct thread thus leads from the Buttes-Chaumont to the electric waterfalls found in major electrotechnical exhibitions. To the notorious technical prowess and imitation of nature, the new electrical exhibitions added an essential element, by staging a new form of greatness. For these symbols, overloaded with modern technology, displayed more than the visible greatness, given the permanent reference to an invisible force or energy. Through these artificial waterfalls and mountains, connected to the production of very real current, the new electric deity imposed itself as the ultimate form of the sublime.

1   See George Kubler, *The Shape of Time: Remarks on the History of Things*, Yale University Press, New Haven 1962.

2   "Beim Betreten des Gebäudes schwelgte das Auge beim Anblick des prächtigen Farbenspiels, welches das in der Auswahl der Blumen und Pflanzen von Meisterhand angeordnete Blumenparkett bildete. Aus der Höhe fiel das bläuliche Licht der Bogenlampen in reichlicher Fülle, an verschiedenen Stellen spielten die Wasserstrahlen durch Scheinwerfer farbig beleuchteter Springbrunnen – ein Bild, das wohl niemand, der es gesehen, jemals vergisst." (Wilhelm Füßl, *Oskar von Miller: 1855-1934, Eine Biographie*, Beck, Munich 2005, pp. 59-60, translated by the author)

3   "Als ich das Zeichen gab, als der Motor sich zu drehen anfing, als die Zentrifugalpumpe wirkte und der Wasserfall zu rauschen begann, entstand eine Begeisterung, von der man sich heute keinen Begriff mehr macht." (Oskar von Miller, "Die geschichtliche Entwicklung der elektrischen Kraftübertragung auf weite Strecken," in: *ETZ* 52 [1931], pp. 1241-1245) See as well Karl Strauss, *Wärmekraftwerke. Von den Anfängen im 19. Jahrhundert bis zur Endphase ihrer Entwicklung*, Springer, Berlin 2016, p. 12.

4   "It is a new century, and what we used to call electricity is its God." (Henry Adams, *Letters 1892-1918*, Cambridge Mass. 1938, II, p. 301)

5   See Kilian Jost, "Ein wahrhaft fabelhafter Anblick," in: *Konstruierte Bergerlebnisse, op. cit.*

6   See Baldine Saint Girons, *Le sublime, de l'antiquité à nos jours*, Désjonquères, Paris 2005.

10

From the Garden to the Alpine Village

One of the most interesting features of the historical series of artificial mountains and their successive meanings is the interplay of echoes, the reception
of older forms that are constantly reborn in new realizations. Thus the second Swiss national exhibition of 1896, in Geneva, theater, inter alia, of a Swiss
village and a "negro village," admired by contemporaries—with, needless to
say, a very imposing mountain built from scratch—takes up and goes beyond
the ephemeral or perennial mounds we encountered along the way.[1] Indeed,
the Geneva event skillfully amplified the topical elements of major national,
universal or electric exhibitions, providing, with its tinkered and assembled
large scale mountain on a site extending from the Plainpalais Plain to the
river Arve, a setting and a spectacular landscape for the entire exhibition. At
the end of the 19th century, the entertainment society was no longer satisfied
with just a grandiose natural setting for visitors, but offered a complete alpine
landscape ready to be admired. In order to make the machine of scenography run, it was necessary to add to the structure set up the authenticity of
an alpine garden, the global visibility suggested by a "Panorama of the Alps,"
but also the plausibility ensured by the presence of the fauna, not to mention
that of the "human fauna": the 350 representatives of Switzerland in flesh and
blood in traditional costume.

Conceived and realized in the heyday of the exhibition movement, the
Helvetic event puts two fundamentally opposed realities side by side: on one
hand, there were most modern machines occupying large halls, an expression of the cutting-edge technology of the time, in particular electrotechnical devices, and the usual variety of encyclopedic pavilions dedicated to the
advancement of industry, agriculture, science, and the fine arts. On the other hand, the Swiss village exhibited the picturesque charm and authenticity
of an entire country, an image conveyed through the miniaturization of the
natural and anthropized territory, with a fake mountain 40 meters high and
almost 600 meters long as its main symbol. Surrounded by heavy palisades
which had to defend the festive space from the possible attack of unem-
ployed people, this landscaped perimeter made it possible to discover three
farms, 56 large houses (*chalets*), 18 smaller ones (*mazots*) and a church, within
a "nature" represented by a 20m waterfall, a stream and a small lake.

NEXT PAGES   The Swiss national exhibition, Geneva 1896, photo: Fred Boissonnas

Presenting the technical-scientific advances alongside the natural aspects, closely linked to the specificity of Switzerland, this exhibition had the intention to be both "national" and universal. The two key concepts underpinning the whole were the machine and the mountain, which cohabited peacefully within a single large, skillfully composed exemplary site. Indeed, on the "natural" side, there is a significant series of components, all related to the mountain theme. First of all, there is the enormous pseudo-mountain, carefully projected and built on site, an alpine scenery reused during the 1900 Paris World's Fair, and also in Dublin, where it was destroyed by fire. At the time of mechanical reproducibility (theorized later by Walter Benjamin), architects, landscape architects and promoters were no longer limited to the representation of the mountain in miniature (in the tradition of the artificial mountain that we are pursuing here), they could finally move it and reuse it elsewhere. Part of the stone molding of the fake Geneva mountain also came from Salève, that is from the nearby Savoyard mountain, in France. As a result, the "Swiss mountains" highlighted and celebrated additionally included materials from abroad. The architecture exhibited in the Swiss village is also intimately linked to the alpine context. As typological objects, the chalets alone already represented metonymically the Alpine territory and the values attributed to this geographical space, at least since the scientist-poet Albrecht von Haller. The miniaturized image of Switzerland as a whole conveyed, in other words, a specifically alpine imagination that favored vernacular architecture close to nature. Here was, just a few meters away from the new electrical, mechanical and cold world (an area in which the Swiss were true pioneers), *another* world that, according to the official exhibition guide, was reminiscent of a "truly Swiss style" or "old Switzerland." We already mentioned the great waterfall and its generous flow, a picturesque *déjà vu* that prolongs both the history of the expositive waterfalls and that of the alpine waterfalls, described and visited by tourists in the 19th century. The waterfall, the stream, the lake, the rock—nothing was missing in the Swiss village of 1896, which also contained the almost secularized version of the aquatic sublime, namely a toboggan hill. In addition, a cave housed the "Panorama of the Alps," in reality that of the Bernese Oberland, previously shown in other exhibition venues.

Finally, the show offered to the countless visitors included two other symbolic objects. The first was an important alpine garden, created by the undisputed master of the genre, Henry Correvon.[2] With this great Geneva specialist, who also collaborated with the landscape architect Jules Alleman on the

Jardin Botanique alpin dela Linnaea à Bourg-St-Pierre "1932
(1690 m altitude)

design of the artificial mountain, we reach the culmination of a fashion that goes back to the tradition of growing medicinal plants on small mountains, mentioned by Olivier de Serres. Also worth mentioning in this context are the "mountain" garden of Montpellier, as well as the rock garden of the Chelsea Physic Garden, from 1772, or the rocks with alpine plants of the Geneva botanist Edmond Boissier, built in 1845. The tradition of arranging alpine plants around or on carefully composed rocks also intersects with that of the rockery specialists. They had erected miniature Mont-Blancs or Matterhorns (for instance at Friar Park, in Henley-on-Thames) and collaborated, as we saw, on international projects such as the Buttes-Chaumont. Correvon transformed the alpine garden into a fashionable object by systematizing the use of plants and proposing, from his Floraire garden in Geneva, models that ranged from the experimental alpine garden realized in its natural context to the "garden terrine" that contained only a few representative plants.

Supported by collectionism, or compulsive accumulation, a characteristic of the second half of the 19th century, the alpine garden spread all over the world. Exhibiting it in 1896 here, on the Plainpalais plain, almost "at home" and close to the nearby Alpine range, represented the crowning achievement of a practice that allowed the mountains to be appropriated in the form of a botanical metonymy. As Correvon was promoting his alpine compositions, he also inaugurated an alpine garden called Rambertia, at an altitude of 2,000m, which was intended to be both a reasoned botanical catalog and a first-rate artistic creation.

ABOVE Alpine garden, Linnaea, Bourg-St-Pierre, Correvon archives

The other symbolic element exhibited in Geneva was a scale model of the Matterhorn made by the great specialist in the field, Xaver Imfeld.[3] This 1:5,000 representation marked the culmination of Swiss craftsmanship that began with the famous reliefs of General Pfyffer in the 18th century. Making miniature mountains is, as we know, an even older tradition, referring both to the Chinese *boshanlu* (see chapter 4) and to the famous *Handsteine*, the precious mounds of the 16th-century goldsmiths. With Pfyffer, the transposition of the relief observed on site to the scale of a readable model became a scientific operation. To accomplish his task, Pfyffer and his successors used mathematical methods and materials technology for three-dimensional rendering.

Moving the Matterhorn from the Valais to Geneva and showing it there, in the city, as a carbon copy, was tantamount to praising this mountain, which has become popular through international mountaineering, and providing an explanation of its special shape. The Matterhorn on a scale of 1:5,000 and the pocket Matterhorns for sale at the exhibition connected this Swiss mountain fair with the valorization exercised, among others, by John Ruskin, who had recognized the Matterhorn as the supreme exemple of the mountain form.

One only has to follow the Matterhorn and its belated discovery as a patriotic mountain to realize that the operation staged in Geneva, in 1896, is more complex and contradictory than the harmonious image it suggested, especially through the propagandist action of the guides and other official publications. We have already witnessed the astonishing fact that the mountain symbol no longer materialized in a single representative object on this

ABOVE *Album de l'Exposition nationale suisse*, Geneva 1896, CIG
OPPOSITE Paris World's Fair, 1900, postcard, n.d.

occasion. At the 1896 exhibition, "the mountain" encompasses different facets: it becomes a plural sign embodied both by the architectural object and by the alpine garden (the alpine plants exhibited in a scientific and aesthetic order), by the "alpine" constructions and the topoi *lake*, *stream*, *waterfall*, *pasture*, *cow*. The support of this symbolic mountain, reduced to a miniature, could now be moved and reproduced with ease. We thus encounter all the elements of the great technopatriotic fair both before and after 1896. The Swiss village of Geneva follows, in fact, the Medieval Village of Turin (1883) and the German Village of Chicago (1893), while the stream-lake-waterfall-mountain system was already in full operation at the Buttes-Chaumont. In addition, a considerable part of the Geneva installations were to be taken up as they were and reused by the same entrepreneurs at the World Exhibition in Paris in 1900. All the components of the great show of 1896 can therefore be moved, quoted, pastiched, and amplified. This equates to a situation where nothing is truly original, whereas the message, conveyed and willingly accepted by the admiring visitors, was the discovery of the original and true Switzerland. The exhibition—and precisely its key setting and concept: the Alpine landscape—thus appears as an extreme artifice, a theatrical assemblage orchestrated by a powerful rhetorical machine. Within this spectacular entirety everything was planned and controlled, including the interplay of polar contradictions and oppositions, for example, between an authentic and patriotic Switzerland on one hand and a technological and avant-garde Switzerland on the other.

The faithful image of Switzerland, "sincere" and "exact," according to the propaganda accompanying the demonstration, ultimately appears to be the result of a gigantic manipulation.

Moreover, it is the cosmopolitan city of Geneva that unveiled a village Switzerland. A closer look to the 1896 national fair shows clearly that everything here was a *trompe-l'oeil*, a mere façade and a simulacrum, starting of course with the Panorama of the Alps. This "greatest landscape ever painted" is part of a series of all-powerful and popular fictions developed from the 19th century across Europe. What mattered, in any case, was for the exhibition machine to generate meaning. The festival, experienced as a great collective performance and made possible by the abolition of the usual distance that separates the spectator from the object of his admiration, ultimately replaced the Ethical Nation by the Aesthetic Nation.

Although prominently political, such a demonstration as that of 1896 is no longer political in the traditional sense of the term. The primacy of the aesthetic aspect, the fact that everything encountered there only spoke to the eyes of the visitors, refers to an ideological operation that very skillfully uses metonymy, the essential stylistic figure of an ephemeral architectural tradition which was so skilled at communicating important messages with symbols such as the mountain. The extent of an entire country was here reduced to a meaningful miniature, to a universe that promised the perfect synthesis between machinist productivism and rustic idyll; between cutting-edge technology and sublime landscape; between being at home and openness to the outside world (primarily in the commercial sense). The model that stood out with this great modern-day fair, marking the pinnacle of the large exhibitions era, was that of a fully controllable and manageable world. In this world regime, everything was in its place, like the peaks of the Bernese Oberland displayed in good order in the "Panorama of the Alps," the chalets arranged in a picturesque way in an ideally "Swiss" village, or the plants carefully assembled in another small, miniaturized universe, namely the alpine garden. The harmonious image of this vision reduced the world to a living canvas, to a topography completely mastered by the human-builder.

This exhibition as a mirror of the world to come can finally be interpreted as an image of an even more worrying situation. Let us not forget that the real promoters of this event were contractors, architects, engineers, and landscapers, i.e. people working in the field of design. However, by providing the irrefutable proof that it was now possible to represent an entire country in miniature, these specialists of the modern world were already indicating, at least in a subliminal sense, the purpose of their ambition: that of transforming the global territory altogether in order to better exploit it.

1   See Jacques Gubler, *Nationalisme et internationalisme dans l'architecture moderne de la Suisse*, L'Âge d'Homme, Lausanne 1975.

2   See Annemarie Bucher, *Von Gärten in den Alpen und Alpen in den Gärten*, in: Christophe Girot, Claudia Moll (ed.), *Aux Alpes, Citoyens! Alpiner Mythos und Landschaftsarchitektur*, Zurich 2005, pp. 11-17.

3   For the history of reliefs see Eduard Imhof, *Bildhauer der Berge. Ein Bericht über alpine Gebirgsmodelle in der Schweiz*, in: *Die Alpen* 57 (1981), pp. 104-166.

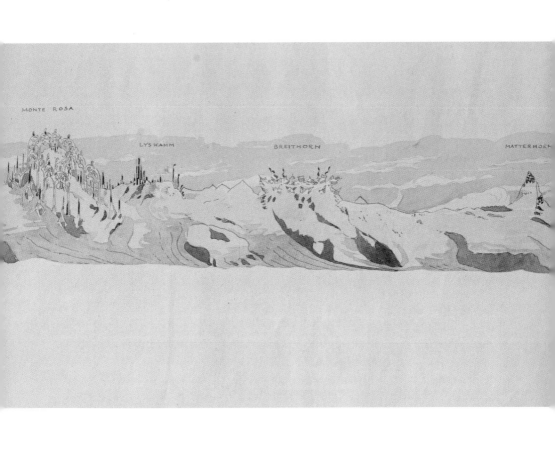

MONTE ROSA   LYSKAMM   BREITHORN   MATTERHORN

ABOVE Bruno Taut, *Alpine Architektur*, Folkwang Verlag, Hagen 1919

11

The crystalline Dream
of utopian Architecture

Once it was imagined and built from the Renaissance onwards, the artificial mountain was linked to the concept of coronation. As a topographical presence, the human-made mountain attracted upwards the gaze of all those positioned below and offered, for those who had access to the summit, a privileged and totalizing view of the world at the foot of the scopic platform. Toward the end of a long historical journey which we have traced by identifying the most significant constructions, we are indebted to the most daring and extravagant vision on this subject to the architect Bruno Taut. The latter starts his architectural mountain projects with a highly symbolic edifice actually erected in 1914, only to surpass it later in the middle of the war period (1917-1918) with two "fantastic" works. The famous *Glashaus*, the "glass house," exhibited between July and August 1914 as part of the great Werkbund event in Cologne, gave thus way to the immensity of the urban project of the *Stadtkrone*, the "City Crown." The third stage and the climax of this itinerary is marked by a singular publication, the *Alpine Archikektur*, "Alpine Architecture," released immediately after the war, in 1919. Apart from the central leitmotif of crystal and crystallization, Taut's triad also has in common the theme of elevation, understood in both a constructive and "spiritual" sense. The Glass House is already, in its own way, a glass mound; the gigantic crystal house that occupies the heights of the visionary city represents a vast architectural mountain; in the *Alpine Architecture*, lastly, the architect becomes the builder of new mountains that raise the majestic chain of the Alps, forming a sublime succession of gigantic crystals.

Given Taut's "social" shift from the mid-1920s and the apparent abandonment of extravagant beauty in favor of functional architecture and urban planning, the two works, intimately linked to the Great War and to a position too quickly identified as "expressionist" or "pacifist," were often relegated to the background. Or, which amounts to the same, they have been categorized as unclassifiable, as "ideal" sketches suitable for the architect's youth, pure exercises of style or, worse still, as the result of the "confusion" due to the lack of mandates and effective work during the war period.[1] We believe that these visionary works and their author do not represent "a dark spot on the map of new architecture,"[2] but, on the contrary, an example to be carefully studied. Such an approach is supported by our main theme, the architectural mountain, convinced as we are that this tradition allows Taut's projects to be

inserted in a more specific context, while the particularity and ambition of the hyperbolic gesture at work in the *Crown City* and *Alpine Architecture* can in turn further illustrate the horizon of the possibilities of mountains erected by man.

Let us therefore logically start with the Glass House. Built on a concrete base formed by a prism with fourteen compartments, the light structure in reinforced concrete culminated in a rhomboid-shaped glass dome. From the entrance of the building, a glass staircase led to the upper part crowned by the dome. The whitish light descending from the top contrasted with the brightness of light from colored lamps. A large opening allowed to descend a second glass staircase down to a waterfall. A golden-colored water streamed through it, while light reflections produced by different tinted glasses gave the whole a kaleidoscopic effect. The room that housed the waterfall had a shining ceiling of gold and silver, the walls were decorated with paintings by different artists, also in glass.

The Glass House combined two essential elements, the crystal (stone) and the waterfall (water). From the outside, it appeared like a large crystal, while inside the interplay of water and light imposed itself. However, both the miniature waterfall and the theme of crystal are intimately linked to the tradition of great exhibitions which, as we know, begin with the famous Crystal Palace in London. Crystal is for Taut, however, much more than a reminder of the glass architecture of major exhibitions. Particularly influenced by the writer Paul Scheerbart, the true champion of glass architecture, and a connoisseur of crystal's staging in important architectural contexts (e.g. at the opening of the Darmstadt artists' colony in 1901), Taut chose this hard and luminous material early on as his favorite symbol. As a form that appears to be a supreme artifice of nature, albeit of natural origin, crystal represents the very image of perfect fusion. Crystal was celebrated in Bruno Taut's time as the synthesis of form and matter, which predestined it to be an ideal model of architecture.

ABOVE Bruno Taut, *Glashaus*, 1914, photographer unknown

By erecting his magic crystal house in the peripheral part of the Werkbund exhibition, Taut created a strong sign that attracted the visitors' attention. His building was intended as a symbolic sign, as the architect himself stated in an article published in 1914, *Eine Notwendigkeit*. He spoke in this regard of a building "which is not only architecture, but in which everything, painting and sculpture, forms a great gesture, and in which architecture merges again with the other arts. Here, architecture must be both the setting and the content. This construction must not pursue a purely practical purpose. Architecture, too, can free itself from utilitarian constraints."[3]

With his crystalline construction, Taut signalized the autonomy of his creative act, making it seem absolute and universal. Hence the intention—although it was actually a pavilion financed by the glass industry and designed as a means of advertising—to renounce all immediate functionality in favor of the atmosphere of this building that glowed lonely, just like a huge crystal. In this context, however, crystal no longer represented a distant original, i.e. mountains or nature; it represented only itself as a concrete and successful synthesis, an artificial nature that had surpassed primordial nature. Humanity was now able to create a form of crystalline architecture without actually imitating nature, and the Glass House was its prototype. This crystal had the magical power to unite everything, even what at first glance contradicted itself: nature and art, technology and poetry. To emerge from the ground as a natural object, when it was actually a calculated and sophisticated architectural composition, was another of the contradictions that Taut's ephemeral house managed to resolve.

The other striking feature of the Glass House, the waterfall, also heralds the skillful diversion of a theme that we have already encountered throughout the history of the artificial mountain (see ch. 8, 9, 10). The only object presented in the central cavity of the large crystal was a source of water, or better, something that looked only remotely like a waterfall. Indeed, everything was done inside this strange house to alter the nature of the water: it was pumped, conveyed, and forced to pass through a series of basins, and it emerged as the main element of a show that favored light. The waterfall is the crystallized water transformed into pure aesthetic performance, thanks to the light and the play of colors reflected in it. However, one should not forget that what made it possible to create such an atmosphere was, in the first place, the invisible power of electricity. The luminous cave in which the visitors descended as in a Chthonian world and the magnificent artificial paradise that surrounded it, were in truth the result of the most advanced technologies of the time. The almighty and Promethean architect was able to master this form of edifying passion and artistic inebriation (*Baulust* and *künstlerischer Rausch*, according to Adolf Behne) because he was in control of almost unlimited building techniques, if compared to the past. Glass, the main material and the main symbol at the heart of the building, is nothing more than a form of modern crystal produced by industry.

45. Stadtsilhouette

The *City Crown*, the second stage of Taut's tripartite ascent, envisions the future urban space as a relationship between the lower city, organized according to the garden city scheme, and a masterful "crown" in the upper part. The latter represents the "spiritual" center of the city (a reality which Bruno Taut considered to be lacking in contemporary cities) and takes the form of a vast glass house whose proportions are not clearly defined. As with the built Glass House of 1914, what counts is the proximity to the Gothic Cathedral, considered to be an impetus towards the sky and a device providing meaning. The Atlas at the beginning of the publication also shows a sample of monuments, mosques, cathedrals, and palaces from all over the world; the common element, including the "crown" built at the top of the city, is the vertical elevation, the will of all these constructions to soar toward the heavens. Admittedly, the height and structure of the crystalline part of the city remain undefined and vague, given that this urban space planned for three million inhabitants was, as far as its extended glass house at the top is concerned, both accessible and inaccessible, feasible and unfeasible. The essential being in this case the crystallization of the general intention of an entire population in a great and marvelous building: "Light wants to pierce the totality of the Whole and it lives in the crystal. Coming from infinity, it settles on the highest peak of the city, it is reflected and shines in the plates, on the edges, on the surfaces and bulges of the crystal house."[4] Imagined during and immediately after the Great War, this luminous and festive vision does little to address the problems of urbanization in the densely populated sphere below. While its horizontal part fits into a harmonious set thanks to the ubiquitous vegetation (following the model of the garden city), the upper part of the city, superlatively magical, is lost in the approximate contours of a construction made of light reflections, shadows and geometric effects. What triggered the imagination of The Crown City, however, was yet another reference, namely the silhouette of the modern city of the 20th century, especially that of New York. The crystal palaces that make up the skyline in the Crown City are the skyscrapers of New York, giant blocks erected using reinforced concrete and glass. Taut's utopia coincides with a brief historical moment during which the modern city, understood as a kind of urban forest in which enormous buildings soar towards the sky like mountain peaks, appears as the horizon of a possible large-scale urbanization. Taut's implicit point of view is, in 1919,

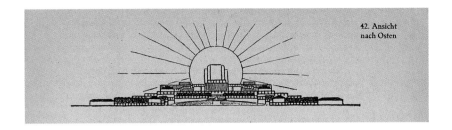

exactly that of the vorticist photographer and painter Alvin Coburn, who rejoiced in the unparalleled scopic power to embrace the entire city made possible by the skyscrapers of his time. Taut contemplated his dream city from an aerial point of view as well, imagining future cities as culminating agglomerations that draw their legitimacy from the "crown" that surmounts them. The analogy between skyskrapers and the mountain is reminiscent of those produced by the effect of Chicago's first high-rise buildings (the Monadnock Building borrows, not coincidentally, its name from the Native American term of a mountain), while anticipating the darker fantasies of Fritz Lang's *Metropolis*, or of a Hugh Ferriss who imagines solipsistic and almost aggressive *Blade Runner*-like mountain buildings. The panoramic presentation of the great universal architecture that closes Taut's book, brings together in a kind of postmodern comic book perspective the history of the architectural sublime with a mountain-building as its culminating expression.

The most immediate opportunity to discover the third stage of Bruno Taut's visionary exploration of the crystalline universe (after the Glass House and the *Crown City*) is to immerse oneself in the beautifully illustrated pages of *Alpine Architecture*. Or better, in simply browsing through this album, which is, again, more reminiscent of the language of comics than of the treatise on architecture. Divided into five parts, the book invites the reader on a walk that takes him step by step away from the terrestrial sphere, already outdated when discovering a new Crystal House (Part I), to the truly cosmic dimension that characterizes the final part, dedicated to the stars. Even more than the previous work, the *Crown City*, *Alpine Architecture* appears as an amalgam of personal elements, reading memories and iconic forms present in the art and architecture of the time. For instance, two of Scheerbart's writings, *Rakkox, der Billionär* (1900) and *Das graue Tuch* (1914) already dealt with the large-scale transformation of a mountain range (in Rakkox's case, the Andes). Taut himself also emphasized his indebtedness to Josef Maria Olbrich, to which one can add that of Peter Behrens and Wenzel Hablik, and the expressionist architectural visions in general.

Finally, with regard to self-referentiality, which is always present in Taut, it should be emphasized from the outset that *Alpine Architecture* begins once again with a house of crystal. Located in the highest region of the Alps, it is only revealed to walkers who have taken upon themselves the extreme effort of a difficult ascent. The construction itself, of disproportionate size, is only characterized superficially in the respective watercolors (this technique

Kristallhaus in den Bergen

3

6

SCHNEE
GLETSCHER
GLAS

Firnen
im ewigen Eise
und Schnee ~
überbaut und ge-
schmückt mit
Umbauungen, Flä-
chen und Blöcken
von farbigem Glase
~ Bergblüten ~

Die Ausführung ist gewiss ungeheuer schwer und opfervoll, aber nicht unmöglich. „Man verlangt so selten
von den Menschen das Unmögliche" (Goethe)

10

ABOVE, OPPOSITE AND NEXT PAGE Bruno Taut, *Alpine Architektur*, Folkwang Verlag, Hagen 1919

Der
Kristallberg

Der Fels ist
oberhalb der
Vegetations-
zone behauen
und geglättet
zu vielfachen
kristallinischen
Formen.

Die hinteren
Schneekuppen
sind mit
Glasbögen-
architektur
bebaut.

Vorne Kristall-
nadelpyra-
miden.

Über dem Ab-
grund eine
Brückenver-
gitterung aus
Glas.

7

makes it possible to suggest more than to illustrate). Apart from the geometrical topography of the existing rocks, elements such as the vault, the staircase, the bridge or the crystal block form a carpet of lines and colors on the page. As in the Glass House, it is still gold and silver that prevail here, everything that reinforces the effect of crystalline brilliance, as well as the arabesque resulting from the decorative mix of neo-gothic glass forms. The waterfall at the Cologne exhibition now reappears infinitely amplified; art (the artificial waterfall) that had replaced nature (the referent waterfall) now attacks Nature itself, the greatest of all, in order to completely and definitively surpass it. The occupation of the Alpine territory as the ultimate site of a totalizing and liberating architecture is moreover one of the main motives of the book from the very beginning.

The only functional part of this alpine crystal palace is limited to a platform to embrace the whole (*Aussichtsbalkon*), where what really counts is to discover the "silence." This monument with a double glass cover, which competes with other nearby peaks, this "temple of silence" is presented as the architectural means to access the *Weltverehrung*, the ultimate mystical and post-romantic symbiosis that would unite, at last, mankind with the whole universe. A fake mountain erected on the back of the real mountain, the gigantic crystal house seems designed to be contemplated either from afar (from a lower region, which makes it even more desirable), or from an even higher vantage point, the aerial viewpoint. "The aerial gaze will change the architecture," says Taut in one of the illustrated pages, "and so will the architects." Other images of the alpine scenario marked by massive human intervention show a crystalline topography where peaks "repaired" or "improved" by the work of builders, attract attention. One thinks of Eugène Viollet-le-Duc and his project to restore the Mont-Blanc summit. Parts II and III, *Mountain Architecture* and *Alpine Construction*, depict a further elevation and an even more brutal modification of Nature. Increasingly imposing glass architectures "bloom" (Taut speaks of *Bergblüten*, mountain flowers) everywhere in the heart of the Alpine region, creating an immense crystalline landscape. The crystal house (already out of scale) is thus metamorphosed into a "crown" that occupies the summits of the Monte Rosa mountain range. The multiplication of glass constructions that adorn peaks like precious jewels, the creation of a completely artificial waterfall that cuts through an entire valley (with water flowing through the building mass, as in F. L. Wright's *Kaufmann House*), the assembly of large crystal blocks that completely occupy another valley, and the epiphany of a mega-crystal—all of this is part of an alpine construction site which deliberately keeps its spatial and temporal boundaries blurred. While the constructive activity should logically affect the entire Alpine chain, its temporal horizon remains open, since in a fictional text by Taut, which proposes a look back on the accomplished *Alpine Architecture* from a future year 1993, the work is still quite ongoing. The author also explains in *Alpine Architecture* that his project is understood as a preliminary to finally access what he calls *das Höhere*, what is

MONTE ROSA BEBAUUNG ~ Glasglocke in gläsernen Streben Bögen und Kristallen

higher. The vaguely metaphysical and mystical orientation, i.e. the search for a post-idealist and post-romantic, non-religious, but aesthetic absolute, should not however make us forget the fact that Taut pursues with this work a clearly defined goal: the mountains to be built were indeed to prevent humanity from repeating what it had done between 1914 and 1918: to kill each other mercilessly. Alongside the superlative beauty, the enchantment of luminous bursts, the symphony of reflections blending with the effects from the wind harps, there was a very simple message here: to replace the destruction caused by war with constructive activity on the largest conceivable scale: the alpine scale. The act of erecting mountains, or even a sequence and a whole repertoire of artificial mountains, artificial waterfalls, artificial crystals, and so on, is no longer conceived as a show. What matters, on the contrary, is the effect and the collective consciousness, the supreme sacrifice made by a humanity that, when it is bored, goes to war (with itself). The limitless building site of *Alpine Architecture* should indeed have been able to pacify Europe, since its population would have participated in a collective effort on the same playground. At a

DER FELS   MATTERHORN < < <

time when the occupation of the Alpine territory was already partially implemented by the hydroelectric industry, by a majestic architecture culminating
in gigantic dams, objects that competed with natural grandeur, Taut opted for
the dreamlike vision of a poetic, political and therapeutic action.

The fact that the artificial architecture, elaborated on the mountain tops,
looks up to the sky already announces the overcoming of the terrestrial perspective. In the final part of the *Alpine Architecture*, the constructions become
partly floating, they are detached from the ground to the sky, like the *Domstern*
(the star-cathedral), a kind of rocket-star architecture. While the night atten-
uates the forms by keeping only the trace of the luminous effects, in the cosmic universe composed of a myriad of worlds, the terrestrial subject reaches
nothingness or the *Namenlose*, that which has no name.

The itinerary staged in Taut's album is based on architectural mountains
that represent the opposite of the metonymic mountain. The Glass House
showed a construction that was already the new crystal (and not its representative) and the urban "crown" did the same in the space of architectural
fiction. Everything becomes visible and adorned thanks to the aesthetic primacy of architecture—which expresses the diktat and the energy of the verbs

at the origin of this activity: *schaffen*, *bauen*, *tun*, whose elevation continues to the infinity of the cosmos. Although *Alpine Architecture* is moving ever further away from the ground and the perspective of what is achievable, several concrete landmarks remain present in the vast crystalline landscape. Taut tackles, in fact, a series of well-known postcard landscapes, starting with the Monte Rosa and Mont Blanc massifs, to the emblematic mountains of Lake Garda or Lake Lugano, and the pre-alpine regions surrounding the Gulf of Portofino, in Liguria.

There is, however, one panel in this series that differs from the others by the minimal intervention of the mountain-building man: it is the illustration dedicated to the *Cervin*, or the Matterhorn, as it is called by Taut, its German name. This famous big boulder is obviously a mountain of a kind: for a long time despised as a "naked" form since it is devoid of vegetation, the Matterhorn was valued in the 19th century by British mountaineers and, above all, by John Ruskin. The latter took the very first photo of the gigantic mountain-rock and discussed its particular beauty in memorable pages of *Mountain Painters*. The Matterhorn was by its prominence the perfect example of a geological form that could have passed for a work of art produced by nature itself. The philosopher Henri Maldiney describes its specificity as follows: "When it appears in the uniqueness of its naked-presence, we are not in sight of a mountain among others, real and possible, and distinguishing itself from them by particular characters, even eminent. Here suddenly an *extremum* opens up in which the whole series is engulfed: the meaning 'mountain' disappears in its significance."[5] It is this significance that attracted Taut's attention. Several of the crystalline mountains erected in the Alps and scattered throughout the boards of *Alpine Architecture* are actually as many Matterhorns. With this mountain, nature may have already fulfilled the architect's dream. However, being a model also entails the danger of trivialization.

Apart from appearing in the picturesque gardens of the 19th century in miniature, or as a relief presented at major exhibitions, this period saw the association of the Matterhorn with a particular product. Indeed, it was in the 1920s that publicist Emil Cardinaux explicitly associated Toblerone chocolate with the Swiss-Italian mountain. From now on it was possible to consume artificial mountains at will, a situation which is not without repercussions on the approach to the real mountains at all. Instead of Taut's "global architecture" in the shape of artificial mountains, there was now a globalized chocolate mountain.

1   Regine Prange, *Das Kristalline als Kunstsymbol, Bruno Taut und Paul Klee*, Olms, Hildesheim 1991, p. 61.

2   *Ibid.*

3   "Das nicht allein Architektur ist, in dem alles, Malerei, Plastik, alles zusammen eine grosse Architektur bildet, und in dem die Architektur wieder in den andern Künsten aufgeht. Die Architektur soll hier Rahmen und Inhalt, alles zugleich sein. Dieses Bauwerk braucht keinen rein praktischen Zweck zu haben. Auch die Architektur kann sich von utilitaristischen Forderungen loslösen." (*Ibid.*, p. 67, translated by the author).

4   "Das Licht will durch das ganze All und ist lebendig im Kristall. Aus der Unendlichkeit kommend fängt es sich in der höchsten Spitze der Stadt, bricht sich und leuchtet auf in farbigen Tafeln, Kanten, Flächen und Wölbungen des Kristallhauses." (*Ibid.*, pp. 97-98, translated by the author).

5   Henri Maldiney, *Cervino*, Tararà, Verbania 2002, p. 4.

ABOVE Construction of the Teufelsberg, Berlin, after 1945

12

History: a Mountain of Debris

An audacious and highly symbolic project developed by the American artist Walter de Maria for the 1972 Munich Olympic Games involved breaking through a mountain of debris from the Second World War. A 122m deep and 2.74m wide shaft would have had to pass through the material accumulated in the Munich mound, without being visible. Only a large metal disc covering this descent downwards and, towards the past, would have indicated the artistic intervention. While the local company responsible, the Olympia-Baugesellschaft, justified its refusal on the grounds that the drilling could have come into contact with military materials and human remains, the abandonment of the *Olympic Mountain Project* is to be interpreted in a more general context, namely the collective amnesia regarding the very existence of such "objects."

The forgetfulness in question is a phenomenon particularly present in post-war Germany, although it reflects a very human attitude. The more humans evolve within a civilization, producing and consuming, the more they will accumulate remnants of varied nature. However, this residual material, which ranges from the fragments of Roman amphoras on the Testaccio in Rome to the countless waste generated by industrial activities and deposited in the slag heaps, normally remains unnoticed. One must be willing to decipher the topography of the world transformed by man to discover that the skin of the earth is strewn with signs that add to its natural structure by creating an artificial topography a sort of carpet of mounds.[1] Artificial mountains that cover the earth's surface are the "positive" mark (in the sense of what is laid down, what is imposed) of "negative" activities (what is generally dug out and not exposed). Moreover, they share the common feature of searching everywhere and always for a zero degree of visibility. This work of camouflage and screening is, furthermore, ensured—even in cases where these objects remain cumbersome or "bizarre"—by nature itself, which, over time, begins to encompass and heal the great "wounds" of anthropic origin.

However, the case of the *Olympic Mountain Project* in Munich appears more complex, given the type of waste in question. What ends, indeed, in the infamous German *Trümmerberge*, the mountains of debris from the Second World War, is not just any or neutral material. It is the entirety of a city, a neighborhood, a street, a house, in short, the totality bombarded and reduced to rubble, forming the contents of these true "mountains of war." Although present in all

major German cities, the emblematic case is obviously that of Berlin. In the German capital, Allied bombing between 1942 and 1945 produced an unimaginable number of debris, and once the war was over, the problem of their evacuation. The mountains of rubble are the tangible result of this evacuation. The presence of these artificial mountains has created a new urban topography in the context of Berlin's flat and undifferentiated landscape. Humboldthain, Friedrichshain, Marienhöhe, Oberbruchkippe, Der Insulaner, Rixdorfer Höhe and a few other luminaries form a small mountain range, which culminates in the famous Teufelsberg.

Located some 17km from the city center in the district of Wilmersdorf, near the Grunewald forest, this focal point of the *Enttrümmerung*, the debris removal, is actually a very special site. Albert Speer, Hitler's megalomaniacal architect-urban planner, had reoriented the city on a new north-south axis, instead of the historical east-west axis, and placed the *Wehrtechnische Fakultät*, the Institute for Advanced Defense Studies, at the head of Berlin's future main axis. It is this powerful symbol of an architecture of perpetual warfare, with its gigantic dome and disproportionate size, this institution which was responsible for the training of the Reich's soldiers, which was to be inscribed in the history of universal architecture as a monument of absolute value. The construction of the Institute for Advanced Defense Studies continued in the midst of the war and resulted in a partially completed structure that resisted even the extremely massive bombardments of the allied forces. Speer, who in his theory of the value of the ruins (*Ruinenwerttheorie*), had clearly indicated that he wanted to erect symbols as imposing as those of ancient Rome, had somehow succeeded in his wager, creating a seemingly indestructible object. The only way to make it disappear was to include it in the "devil's mountain" for which it served, in part, as a base.

The actual construction of the Teufelsberg took 25 years. The new mountain accumulated during this period about 26 million m³ of debris, creating an object twenty times larger than the Pyramid of Giza. The project, which obviously interested all the successive administrations of the city of Berlin (the architect Hans Scharoun had a central role in it for a year, from 1945 to 1946), was carried forward by the landscape architect Reinhold Lingner. His main idea, as he explained in 1950, was to take the rubble out of the city and dispose of it in places where the glacial geology was particularly suitable for the construction of a new large-scale topography. The dislocation of the debris should have been followed, according to him, by a greening work, which was to ensure at the end of the course the transformation of the completed mountains into parks or forests. Like Berlin's other mountains of debris, the Teufelsberg was made by slowly filling the empty center from the outside in. At the end, the topsoil, transported from Bremen, added a final layer that covered the amorphous mass, ensuring rapid greening. The mythology of the *Trümmerfrauen*, the women who worked in debris removal, was another significant element of this coverage and "normalization" strategy. While less than 5% of the workforce were female, it was the image of the woman in the midst of the fragments of the war that imposed itself on posterity. The staging of female protagonists popularized the image of fragile people using their hands to face the hard, dangerous and cold matter. The elaboration of a whole technical lexicon related to Trümmer (*Trümmerbahn*, *Enttrümmerung*, etc.) also contributed to give the titanic activity of the complete evacuation of the war scraps a more neutral and technical aspect. The names of the new mountains: grove (*Hain*), plateau (*Höhe*), belvedere (*Blick*)... point in the same direction; they fit perfectly into the picturesque tradition. If history in general resembles, according to Walter Benjamin, a *Trümmerhaufen*, a heap of debris, then the major activity of Germany in the *Wiederaufbau* period, accelerated reconstruction, consisted in the evacuation of its recent history. Now, how can history be cancelled out if not by making it disappear in an ex-territorial object, or, which amounts to the same thing, in an object that merges with nature itself?

Moving the debris to the outskirts of the city, out of sight, already allowed during the immense construction site, which lasted a quarter of a century, to forget the ruinous state of the post-war landscape. The quasi-ex-territoriality of these areas, which were filled with the remains of what was once Berlin, Cologne, Frankfurt, or Munich prepared the way for a final pacification, accomplished once the rubble mountains were filled in and ready to be landscaped. Natural camouflage completed the displacement by offering visitors a landscape of great banality. Walking, picnicking, using the slide, flying kites and so on—all this happened here "naturally" within a site that also seemed perfectly natural.

One of the effects of this strategy of evacuation and occultation is the topographical non-relation between the artificial mountains and the city they "crowned," without it really mattering to the latter. The disconnection and active forgetfulness of the past, thus created in Berlin and elsewhere in Germany the opposite of what can be defined as a place of memory. The artificial mountains were certainly prominent, but they had nothing to say. With the grass and shrubs growing, it was as if Nature herself wanted to forgive the past, to forget the catastrophe of war. Reinhold Lingner in particular tried to

legitimize himself by using a specific landscape narrative. He was keen to emphasize respect for nature, the relationship with local geology, knowledge of flora, the effect of nature on physical well-being, he spoke of "biomorphism," and similar concepts. However, it should never be forgotten that landscape architecture is not a "neutral" discipline. It is, on the contrary, linked in the German case to an ideology that had an important impact in all areas of life during the Third Reich. The contrast between the enormity of the action set up under the label of *Enttrümmerung* and the nullity of what appears on site with the artificial mountains is actually the result of a project skillfully orchestrated and made possible by a camouflage-like landscaping. The landscape architecture project and the intention to allow as quickly and efficiently as possible the fusion with Nature explain why these mountains are so lacking, until today, of inscriptions, disturbing traces, visible wounds, but also simple explanations. Instead of any exegesis, these artifacts, which are out of scale and could have been significant, are limited to providing a smooth, green, ordinary and neutral image of nature. The mountains of debris, in Berlin and elsewhere, are just *another* landscape or, worse, a harmless playground.

The strategy of the "mountains of debris" operation represents, in some ways, a success. It has effectively rid German cities of their cumbersome remnants and created a topography that generally eludes sight and awareness. It also functioned as a life-size laboratory to test the possibility of growing vegetation on the crest of these huge piles of mineral origin. The transformation of

---

the top of the debris mountains into forests, actively implemented by Lingner and his collaborators, anticipates a current trend regarding the metamorphosis of dump sites into forests.[2] If we move away from the superficial image of mountains of debris, we must admit that we had to wait for a project proposed by an American artist in the 1970s, or a study combining anthropology and a personal statement by an Australian researcher[3], in 2017, to confront what remains deposited inside these fake mountains. The landscape of the German debris mountains is the opposite of the landscape imagined by Bruno Taut. While the construction of the sublime mountains crowning the Alps should ideally have prevented the war, the war generated during the reconstruction a set of very large mounds of extreme dullness.

Within the debris mountains, however, the compacted and displaced history is still present. To ignore it is equivalent to cultivating a form of non-relation that culminates, precisely, in those non-monuments that persist in saying nothing. Everybody knows, however, that this new geography is far from natural, but as long as these very special mountains remain marginal, the status quo seems to be maintained. Although silent and distant, these objects remain the symbol of a process that characterized the (German, but not only) post-war reconstruction. The starting point is, if we take a step back, the existence of a historical architectural heritage, namely the built universe of cities. In Berlin and elsewhere, the bombing destroyed a large part of the built heritage, leading to an undifferentiated field of debris at the end of the war. This radical negation of the city, which almost no longer existed as a form, demanded a new constructive stage, the *Enttrümmerung*. But unlike restoring buildings or building *ex novo* in the city, the action leading to the rise of the mountains of debris did not actually build anything at all: it was limited to moving and accumulating. The rubble mountain is therefore not a construction, it is only the support and the platform—certainly imposing—of the staging of a fictitious nature that favors forgetfulness.[4]

1   See Alan Berger, *Drosscape: Wasting Land in Urban America*, Princeton University Press, New York 2007.

2   See Niall Kirkwood, *Manufactured Sites. Rethinking the Post-Industrial Landscape*, Taylor & Francis, London 2001.

3   Benedict Anderson, *Buried City, Unearthing Teufelsberg: Berlin and its Geography of Forgetting*, Routledge, London 2019.

4   The fate of the Wehrtechnische Fakultät is also non-dialectical. This solemn block and symbol of the III. Reich built in the middle of the war survives intact inside the false mountain which became its tomb. It is covered by the debris produced by the logic that was to be propagated by the Wehrtechnische Fakultät.

ABOVE Disneyland Matterhorn, Anaheim, n.d.

The world's most visited Matterhorn is not in the heart of the Alps. It is in Southern California, in Disneyland, that a fake mountain bearing the same name continues to attract the attention of millions of people each year. The genesis of the Anaheim Matterhorn, inaugurated on June 14, 1959 by Walt Disney and Vice President Richard Nixon, is the result of the meeting of several distinct factors. The local starting point for the future big Disneyland attraction was a large garbage heap located between two major thematic hubs in the entire amusement park, *Fantasyland* and *Tomorrowland*. *Fantasyland* already contained elements of the Alpine pseudo-vernacular, while *Tomorrowland*, the sphere of the conquest of space, allowed to imagine the exploration of extraterrestrial "mountainous" areas. The residual material from the creation of the *Sleeping Beauty Castle*, which had remained on site since 1956—a common custom in countless sites around the world, characterized by a lack of interest for what did not directly serve the main attraction—and accumulated in a mound, was considered a foreign element that contrasted ostensibly with the well-kept appearance of the ensemble. Flattened, covered with topsoil, planted with a few trees and equipped with benches, this small remnant not assimilated by the enchanting totality was disturbing. Used by lovers and solitary picnickers, the small artificial mountain took, ironically, the name of *Looking Mountain* (the summit was some 6 meters high) or *Holiday Hill*.

   The second constituent factor contributing to the construction planned at a certain moment with the name Mount Disneyland (thus signaling the desire to create much more than a simple geographical reminder) was the presence of Walt Disney in Switzerland, and particularly in Zermatt, during the shooting of the documentary *Switzerland First* and, in 1958, of the mainstream film *The Third Man on the Mountain*. The discovery of the "real" site and the sucessful cinematic use of the Matterhorn motivated Disney to permanently demolish *Holiday Hill* and replace it with a new, extraordinary mountain. Legend has it that Disney sent a postcard with the Matterhorn to his "Imagineers" (his specialists in the layout and landscaping of choosing subjects within the theme park), containing the message: "Build it!" The idea of reproducing the Italian-Swiss original, admired on site, contrasts, however with the circulation of a series of names for the future mountain that anticipate the project of the Californian Matterhorn. The very fact of hesitating between *Snow Hill*, *Snow Mountain*, *Magic Mountain*, *Fantasy Mountain*, *Echo Mountain*, and *Disneyland*

Mountain is significant in terms of the identity of the created mountain. Yet, is it really a Matterhorn?

The third factor, finally, is the search for a suitable site for a revolutionary roller coaster technology. The presence of slides and a bobsled track inside and outside the mountain to be built, to which were added gondolas, was to immediately transform the discovery of this mountain into a kinetic adventure. The rapid movement of the bobsled on a steel structure was intended to make the mountain experience more dynamic, giving it both the prestige of speed and the sequential and narrative structure characteristic of the cinematic language.

The inauguration of the Matterhorn Disney version was celebrated as a second birth of Disneyland. The new attraction provided—just like the panoramas of the 18th and 19th centuries—a completely new experience of the mountain, based on an artifact that replaced or even surpassed the original. At Disneyland, the visitor could see the mountain-object of desire from afar (it was even the first visual element to be seen when exiting the Santa Ana Freeway), he would approach it, and then explore it from the outside and the inside. To the usual welcome of "the mountain," that of tourists, hikers, and mountaineers, the Disney Matterhorn added, at least apparently, a more direct, more wholesome, and more exciting experience. In order to create this effect, important financial and human resources were committed. From the outset, the method underlying the project also included not only a replica of the Matterhorn, but the creation of another Matterhorn, the technological "Disneyland Matterhorn." It is very significant in this context that the attempt to represent this very well-studied, measured, and modeled mountain was based on an almost naive and tinkered "translation." Ignoring the scientific

---

ABOVE Walt Disney with a scale model of the Disney Matterhorn,
Los Angeles Herald Examiner, Photo Collection, 1958

reliefs and even the Matterhorns in miniature, sold at international exhibitions, the Disney collaborators proceeded instead of inventing their own methods of reproduction along the way. Harriet Burns, who built the first models in the WED Model Shop, explains it very well: "We had a few illustrations from *National Geographic*, a double-page from *Life* and two postcards—virtually nothing."[1] Her remark that "today they would bring in people to measure everything carefully etc., but we had none of these means,"[2] testifies not to the lack of means at the time, but rather to the willingness not to use them. For what mattered was not to rebuild the Matterhorn, but to build this *other* Matterhorn.

The realization of the mountain went through several stages of modeling. A first small Matterhorn of about 30cm in clay was built like a pastry, layer after layer.[3] The next model already had a metal skeleton to integrate waterfalls and the rudimentary roller coaster system. Once the clay was replaced by plaster, the five copies of this mini-Matterhorn were landscaped using the techniques of model making (even a small train passed inside). In order to erect the 147-foot fake mountain (which amounts to a reduction of 1:100, the Matterhorn measuring 14,700 feet), the Imagineers cooperated with a team of top engineers. American Bridge was responsible for the production of the steel structure, the gigantic endoskeleton composed of 2,175 elements, each of different length and shape. The metal framework was covered with plywood and cement, to serve as a support for the elaboration of the "skin" to simulate the "rockery," the rocky material of the mountain. One of the most effective ways to ensure the likelihood of the result was a painting. The blue-grey-silver "character paint" successfully imitated a reinvented Alpine landscape in a park setting in sunny southern California.

The Anaheim Matterhorn is the result of considerable landscaping work. Real pine trees of different sizes, kept alive by a watering system, fake chalets, partly recovered from the Alps and reassembled on site, fake waterfalls and fake glaciers formed a heterogeneous but coherent ensemble. The seduction operation made possible by this imposing object—its height corresponded to that of a fourteen-story building—was not intended to transport the visitor to the vague and distant elsewhere of the European Alps. The *elsewhere* simulated by the mountain aimed at a place erected right here, in the recent but important tradition of the technological sublime made in USA—that is to say an elsewhere imagined on the basis of on site experience. The mountain, reduced to a scale that best served the overall philosophy of the theme park, actually functioned as a "weenie,"[4] a catch for visitors to be enchanted by a

ABOVE Disneyland Matterhorn, Anaheim, advertising, n.d.

ABOVE Structure of the Matterhorn, Anaheim, 1959

ABOVE   Construction of the Matterhorn, Anaheim, 1959

machine designed down to the last detail. Home to the superlative spectacle of the time, the ultra-fast bobsled, this mountain, never replicated in the other parks of the group, represented the top of the Disney system between 1960-1970. Like the large park that surrounds it, the Matterhorn was a huge empty shell ready to be filled with increasingly sophisticated scenic features, or to be perpetually transformed. This mountain without mass and true mountain content was intended to be occupied and adorned by scattered signifiers such as "glacier," "lake," or "yeti" ("the abominable snowman"), which corresponded to pseudo-vernacular themes. It thus served, from the outset, as a physical and conceptual framework for a virtual reality that could be easily manipulated by Disney designers. Emptying the mountain from the mountain while guaranteeing, on the surface, its shape, fully corresponded to the logic of the consumer society of the time. This mountain did not present itself as such: it appeared, on the contrary, as an empty container that allowed the image of the mountain to be presented, an image thematically divided, as in children's books.[5] Through this Matterhorn, the image had reached such a power that it managed to completely replace the "real" mountain that had become old-fashioned. The real thrills resulting from the "encounter" with the mountains were those experienced in Disneyland and no longer the thrills experienced in the mountains, now explored and accessible to everyone.

However, the mountain of Anaheim is not an object deprived of referents. The first one, omnipresent and attractive, is the very concept of the mountain. This Matterhorn, which appeared in 1959, signifies, in other words, the triumph of self-reference. It *is* actually Mount Disneyland, the mountain that absorbs the park just as the park absorbs the mountain. It functions as an irresistible here-and-now, thanks to a form of reception that can rightly be called extreme. Located in an enclosed and self-sufficient space, this mountain forcefully attracts a new type of "pilgrims" who accept the disappearance of the real world during the indeterminate time of their visit to Disneyland. To penetrate this artificial mountain, is equivalent to discovering an architectural and carefully decorated signifier that never ceases to speak of the signifier "Disney." The park and its main attraction, the Matterhorn absorbs the world in its entirety, demonstrating the replacement of all possible geographies and stories by an oversimplified narrative.

Finally, there is an important difference between the discovery of this mountain, built by modern engineers, and the experience related to the artificial mountains of the past. All the previous constructions were, as we have seen, presented in frontal or *vis-à-vis* situations. Admittedly, the mounds of Ferrara, Rome, Pratolino or Wörlitz also concealed caves, which made it possible to explore both the external face and an often-mysterious interior. The great exhibitions of the 19th century obviously created a fairground atmosphere, which gave the daring constructions erected by engineers, landscapers and rock climbers a distinctive magic. However, all of these experiments were carried out on foot. This established a relationship between the observing subject and the observed attractions, subject to the rhythm of the people walking. At Disneyland, on the contrary, visitors discovered most of the attractions while sitting in a vehicle. Experiencing the mountain in bobsled had several decisive consequences. It considerably reduced the distance between the visitor and his object of desire, exposing him to a situation in which he was almost totally merged with the surrounding environment, which metamorphosed him. The safety of the brand-new roller-coaster system (traveling in light metal vehicles instead of the old wooden ones) created the conditions for a smooth and "natural" ride, which made people forget about everything else outside this total experience. Moreover, with its "magic mountain" Disneyland inaugurated a new chapter in the history of the sublime. Indeed, the discovery of the Matterhorn combined terror, due to the speed, the size of the pseudo-massif, and the extreme pleasure of being the privileged participant of this kind of adventure, all made possible thanks to a gigantic representation. The commercial sublime also benefited from the eminently cinematic quality of this Matterhorn experience. Not only in and around the mountain, but within the theme park, in general, visitors moved around as if in a traveling shot, during a show that never ended.[6] To get to know and fully admire a mountain, you had now to stay in motion and use spectacular viewpoints, and that is exactly what Disneyland offered to any visitor willing to pay for this kind of adventure.

1   Jason Surrell, *The Disney Mountains: Imagineering at Its Peak*, Disney Editions, 2007, p. 15 (translated by the author).

2   *Ibid*. (translated by the author).

3   *Ibid*., p. 16.

4   Walt Disney liked to pretend to be someone who knew how to attract people, as one would do with a dog seduced by a sausage (*wiener = weenie*) stretched on a pole.

5   The fictional collage was crude. During the first decade the metal structures were visible: the visitors were aware that they were discovering a construction.

6   Thibault Clément, *Plus vrais que nature. Les parcs Disney ou l'usage de la fiction dans l'espace et le paysage*, Presses Sorbonne Nouvelle, Paris 2016.

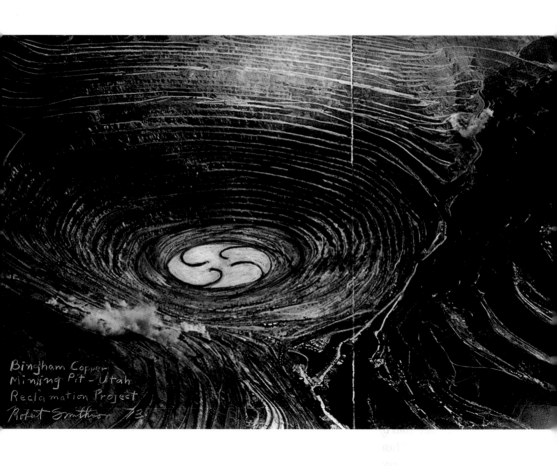

ABOVE   Robert Smithson, *Reclamation Project*, 1973, ©Holt/Smithson Foundation/
VAGA at Artists Rights Society (ARS), NY

Around the time the construction of *Space Mountain* in the *Magic Kingdom* of the Walt Disney Corporation in Florida began in 1971—an attempt to repeat the success of the Californian Matterhorn—the American artist Robert Smithson imagined the realization of an "underground cinema." Located in a cave, an abandoned mine or in a post-industrial site, this cinema unlike any other should have occupied the interior space of a large underground cavity. *Towards the Development of a Cinema Cavern or the Movie Goer as Spelunker* represents, in a way of thinking typical for Smithson, the synthesis between the science fiction of the time, popularized and staged, among others, in Walt Disney theme parks, and mythical places such as Plato's cave. The "cinematic atopia" envisioned by the artist wanted to put an end to the "immobilization of the body" typical of the spectator's situation in the cinema, as well as to a receptive state close to "coma." The experience in the cave intended, on the contrary, to awaken people sitting on rocks, to transpose them to another time-space, far from certainties and canonical habits. Such a device would have worked, if implemented, with an effect similar to that of the sequences offered in Disney's theme park, while nevertheless questioning the certainties of the usual psychological comfort zone and shaking the viewer from top to bottom (Smithson considered "any art form dangerous both mentally and physically").[1]

The rocky and secluded setting of the Cinema Cavern is reminiscent of the structure of several other works, actually realized or only imagined by Smithson. What they have in common is, even at first glance, the frequent recourse to the artificial mountain. Whether it is *Broken Circle/Spiral Hill*, *Asphalt Spiral*, *1,000 Tons of Asphalt*, *Map of Broken Glass*, *Gravel Mirrors*, *Mirror Strata*, *Island Project*, *Museum of the Void*, and so on—all of these objects, which are otherwise not easy to define, vary the theme of mound, heap, mass layered or filled with debris. They accumulate various materials, glass, asphalt, crystals, earth or rocks, with a clear relationship to geology, archaeology, or history, i.e. to an understanding of the physical world as a reality produced over a long period of time.

Smithson has a predilection for this complex shape, without ever opting for an archetypal symbol or an element that would pass as his brand image. What characterizes his works is "an attempt to move away from a specific object. My objects are constantly moving to a different area. They cannot be isolated since they are on the run."[2] The mountain form as he conceives it is neither

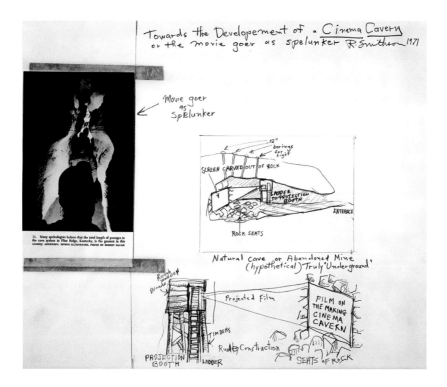

stable nor stabilizable. Nor is it the expression of a successful *Aufhebung*, in the sense of crowning and containing all the faux mountains built in the past; rather, it imposes itself within a route that does not end with it. Indeed, the artist opens and dislocates the history that precedes him, redefining and over-complicating it. By favoring the artificial mountain, he connects with older practices, while his own proposals are never exhibited as the culmination of a series.

The emergence of Smithson's work comes at a historic moment of profound transformation in the domain of artistic practices—particularly in the field of sculpture. In a landmark article, Rosalind Krauss analyzed the transition from sculpture synonymous with monumentality and rootedness to a situation characterized by "the absolute loss of place."[3] In this new constellation, sculpture—malleable and strange—became self-referential or "pure negativity." The new terms "site construction" or "marked sites" reflect this paradigm shift that sets the stage for Smithson's major innovations.

Two important precursors paved the way for Smithson and his colleagues' interventions in the context of what would later be defined as Land Art (even if the more correct term would be Earthworks or Earth Art). The first is Isamu Noguchi, who used childrens' playgrounds as an experimental field of choice. Decided to simplify and improve the use of the playground, while improving its aesthetic qualities, Noguchi elaborated several remarkable models. *Play*

ABOVE Robert Smithson, *Towards the Development of a Cinema Cavern or the Movie Goer as Spelunker*, 1971, ©Holt/Smithson Foundation/VAGA at ARS, New York

Mountain (1933), *Contourned Playground* (1941) and
United Nations Playground (1952) all used the ability
to shape a topography that combined concave and
convex, the strict geometry of straight lines and
curves. These never built projects, whose models
were revealed in various exhibitions, represent a
sophisticated blend of sculpture, art, architecture,
and landscape architecture. The idea of "sculpt-
ing" a children's playground must have confused
specialists whose practice was based on following
well-established standards, and for whom aesthetics was of little importance. The subversive side of
Noguchi's playgrounds was precisely concerned
with aesthetic quality, as well as considerations
related to a certain conception of safety. The pyramids, mounds, steps, triangles, rectangles, and
other forms integrated in these landscapes and the
rhythm resulting from the amalgamation of these
freely composed elements marked, in any case,
only a relative negation of the existing. Indeed,
these projects, once built, could have worked very
well since they responded first and foremost—and
better than standardized solutions—to the physical
demands of the human body, such as climbing, descending, jumping, walking, exploring. Noguchi's
"play sculptures" were, in other words, plural objects ready to be fully integrated into the respective
urban context.

The second most significant case, upstream of
Smithson's works, is Herbert Bayer's *Grass Mound*
(1954) and *Marble Garden* (1955) in Aspen, Colorado.
The grassy mountain consists of a ring of earth approximately 13m in diameter with a mound inside, a large white rock, and a
small furrow. Erected in front of the Aspen Institute for Humanistic Studies,
its photograph was shown in the famous 1968 *Earthworks* exhibition (the first
public appearance of what was to become Land Art). The *Marble Garden*, on
the same site in Aspen, consists of a large platform with a small pond, a geometrical plan on which large blocks of marble of different size and shape create
a surprising effect of shadows and lights. This "garden" also used the residual
material from a disused quarry with unpolished marble blocks. Although they

RIGHT, TOP TO BOTTOM Isamu Noguchi, *United Nations Playground*, 1952; Isamu Noguchi, *Play Mountain*, 1933; Herbert Bayer, *Grass Mound*, Aspen, 1954; Herbert Bayer, *Marble Garden*, Aspen, 1955, Aspen Historical Society

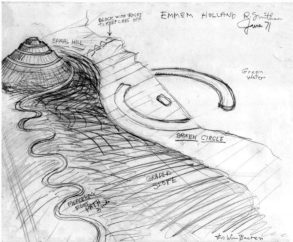

were pioneering works that challenged the usual divisions between garden, landscape, architecture and sculpture, Bayer's two creations nevertheless remained decorative. They certainly conveyed the typical spirit of a Bauhaus aesthetic, in which Bayer had played a central role, without creating the sense of disorientation that would characterize Smithson's projects.

A brief tour of Smithson's journey on the theme of the artificial mountain will, on the contrary, allow us to understand the degree of innovation and the subversive quality of his works, a characteristic lacking in other artists of the time using the mountain as a form of expression and reflection. Let us start with *Spiral Hill*, a 23-meter-high spiral mound made in 1971 in Emmen, Netherlands. What was originally a "bare" earth construction appears today as a small mountain covered with vegetation. The mountain part is inseparable from the *Broken Circle*, a sand pier, approximately 40m in diameter that surrounds a huge rock. Located on the shores of a small lake, the circle divided in two, marks the boundary between land and water. This double installation, *Broken Circle/Spiral Hill*, his only surviving earthwork outside the United States, occupies the site of an abandoned sand quarry. Like most of the artist's creations, it is located in a peripheral zone marked first by industrial exploitation and then by the end of all activity. Thought in a long-time frame, the active industrial phase represents only an extremely brief moment, however. What is more, talking about a shutdown also appears to be a simplification, since the site will continue its "life" in an ever-changing form.

Introducing this site by proposing the perspective of an artificial mountain thus consists in creating the conditions of possibility of a change of perspective. By climbing *Spiral Hill*, one was invited to look at the reality of this place in a different way. The climb is, as its name suggests, spiralic, with a spiral that

TOP LEFT   Robert Smithson, *Spiral Hill for viewing Broken Circle*, Emmen, Holland, 1971; TOP RIGHT   Robert Smithson, untitled drawing of *Broken Circle/Spiral Hill*, 1971, both images ©Holt/Smithson Foundation/VAGA at ARS, New York

turns left, in the "wrong direction." For Smithson, turning left is not linked to a religious tradition, but to the key concept of his artistic poetics: entropy. Entropy, a concept derived from thermodynamic theory, emphasizes the fact that natural processes tend to move irrevocably, at a given moment, from a state of order to a state of disorder. Other than the mechanistic explanation of the world, entropy privileges chaos and disorder, which distinguishes it from all forms of the myth of progress. Entropy is evolution in reverse. However, in Smithson's very personal interpretation, there are both negative and positive aspects linked to entropy. One can name on the negative side the excessive energy that characterizes 20th century civilization, a state of overheating that often announces (as science-fiction of the 1960s and 1980s, for example, indicates) catastrophe. The positive aspect lies, however, in the fact that nature itself is, and always has been, entropic. Smithson therefore decided, as he puts it, to "collaborate with entropy," which means to be interested in everything that is unfinished, impure, and marginal.

Considering entropy does not correspond to a passive or nihilistic attitude. Smithson never stops erecting, building, assembling, moving, multiplying projects. Instead of adopting a particular ideology and therefore a unilateral position as an artist, he thought he was acting rather as a mediator between the extremes of consumerist ("sadistic," in his words) and ecological ("hysterical," in his words) attitudes. It is true that many of his works will be created in areas that represent white spots on the map; occupying them, he has nevertheless erected—as in Emmen—objects of remarkable size and aspiration, although fragile and exposed to time.

In this context, the spiral mountain appears as a polysemic element worthy of attention. The spiral is inseparable from the history of science and the history of art: just think about its role in Leonardo da Vinci—both in his theory of fluids and in the representation of tresses of hair—or in Dürer, who thematized it in his 1525 *Underweysung*. The counterclockwise spinning spiral raises a fundamental question about natural history: does the universe spin in the right direction? Does it follow a direction? Does it have a meaning? Since Smithson favors polysemy, and all certainty seems broken, his artwork does not really take a clear position, but rather "collaborates" with the entropic forces. Ultimately, it is up to the visitor to form an opinion, by climbing *Spiral Hill* and arriving at its platform. It is by looking from top to bottom at this highly artificial topography, which combines sculpture, architecture, art, and landscape architecture, that he will have to reflect and orient himself. What is essential here is the open and undefined aspect of the journey, reflecting the instability of the installation, which changes, as does the existence of the visitors or the universe itself. Arriving at the top, the size of the erratic block integrated into the project can be measured more than by walking and perceiving it in the horizontal perspective. This rock (reminiscent of its predecessor in Aspen), one of the largest in the Netherlands, could not be moved. Its presence—a source of disturbance and questioning—was an element included

in a second phase of the project since it very well corresponded with the ideas the artist wanted to highlight.

Without taking the form of a massive artificial mountain, other works by Robert Smithson also exploited aspects of the mountain understood as a reality resulting from specific processes, whether geological or anthropogenic. The various "spills" staged in the 1969-1970, for example, used the declivity of slopes, hillsides, or gullies to organize the slow flow of materials in relation to the building industry. Whether asphalt, industrial glue, cement or mud— each spill created a powerful and deformed material trail exposed to time. *Asphalt Rundown* (1969), the best known of these ephemeral works, was installed in a disused quarry on the outskirts of Rome. Once the asphalt was poured, it slowly dragged down the slope from the glutinous to the solid state, from hot to cold, an obvious metaphor for the Second Law of Thermodynamics (regarding entropy). Metamorphosing into a crust covering the slope of the quarry, the asphalt was exposed to the elements until its dissolution and final disappearance. The same thing happened with the glue poured into a ravine in Vancouver: the industrial product, transported to the site and released by a large truck, began an unpredictable journey, assuming a provisional form that gradually led to its complete erasure.[4] The temporal aspect of this type of intervention is obvious: the material used was reminiscent of the distant—geological—origin of its components and the more recent time of its manufacture; the action highlighted the moment of overturning, the crystallization of the still malleable form, and the moment of hardening. Added was the decomposition of the mass that covered the site for a given period of time, as well as the moment of the photographic representation of the intervention. These kinds of artistic actions, seemingly simple despite their size and cost, raise many other questions, for example, those related to gravity, geomorphology or the genesis of the stacked and stratified forms found on the earth's surface. Rather than dealing with historical time—the conceptual category that served as an interpretative horizon for the European artistic tradition—Smithson favored, as he frequently pointed out, geological time. With his open-air experiments organized away from museums, art galleries and inhabited places, he created installations that deal with the question of the origin of mountains, the formation and flow of

ABOVE Robert Smithson, *Glue Pour*, Vancouver, 1969, ©Holt/Smithson Foundation/ VAGA at ARS, New York

A heap of language

lava, as well as the possibility of reading the processes of the past in the strata of what is sediment.

The gesture of the spill clearly mobilizes the image of the civilization of waste, whose naive phase reached its peak in the 1970s, just before the oil crisis. Tens of thousands of trucks transport—a worldwide activity that continues to our days—waste to marginal areas, inexorably creating impressive mounds, some of which, like the famous New York landfill at Fresh Kills, Staten Island, have grown to considerable size. Along with his artist friends Nancy Holt, Robert Morris, and Carl Andre, Smithson has systematically explored the world of pits, quarries, garbage dumps, and disused sites over the years in search of suitable locations for his interventions. The trace left during a period (obviously entropic) by industrial glue, asphalt or cement, a phenomenon resulting from the edifying action of man, is, while being deformed, nevertheless legible. It inscribes on the back of a mound or slope the presence of something fundamentally strange, of a material that is out of control and disturbing. "Reading" such a work is not so different from reading a text, at least if one considers reading as the search for the deeper meaning of an enunciation. Compared to the traditional language of art, and especially of European art marked by iconography, iconology and the search for sources, i.e. by *logos*—the act of assembling artificial mountains or spills (Smithson, in this respect, willingly used the term *alogos*) seems at first glance almost primordial and devoid of intertextuality. However, if one understands these actions in their dual relationship with the natural history of the earth and the industrial past, everything immediately appears more complicated and requires further hermeneutic reflection. A work such as *A heap of language* from 1966, highlights the parallels between Smithson's "sculptural" manifestations and the act of writing. Or to say it with him: "Words and rocks contain a language that follows a syntax of fragments and breaks."

ABOVE Robert Smithson, *A heap of language*, 1966, ©Holt/Smithson Foundation / VAGA at ARS, New York

"Stare at any word long enough and you will discover a series of faults, a field of particles, each containing its own nothingness."[5] By piling up words, the artist is forced to descend into the "mountain" of language, where each word contains crevices and reveals one subterranean stratum after another. Thus the series included within *A heap of language* begins with the word "language" and continues with "phraseology speech/tongue lingo vernacular/ mother tongue, King's English/dialect [...]."[6] By stacking material, or pouring it on the side of a mound, actions that follow projects conceived by Smithson's avalanche-like imagination ("my thoughts are like an avalanche in my mind")[7], the artist did the same: he demanded a reading of his work from the surface to the deepest strata.

Smithson's works in exhibition spaces also touch on different aspects of the mountain. In these cases too, samples of material—earth, glass, rock, gravel, crystal...—are reminiscent of the typical cataloguing of geological samples in natural science museums or various collections through the arrangement in boxes. The actual presence of materials taken from distant and often inaccessible places is accompanied by photographic and cartographic documentation. The logic of the *Nonsite* (this is the term used by the artist for works that represent a distant material reality, in 3D) intends, in any case, to break the habits and conceptual barriers, recalling the relativity and interrelation of the usual distinctions such as interior/exterior, here and there, original/copy, and so on. Samples from elsewhere, moved and collected in the context of an art gallery, require translation, a process of relating what at first glance seems completely separate. The *Nonsites*, fundamentally abstract and conceptual works, thus appear to be composed of both the "here" exposed and an "elsewhere" to imagine. Moreover, Smithson further complicates its installations by often using mirrors. Both support and optical element, the mirror leaning against a rock or crossing a gravel heap reveals the cluster in a split form, introducing an additional layer to the relationship between "here" and "there."

Everything "here" is at the same time a "there," everything is only an entropic flow, and this is also true for apparently solid and compact matter. As in a literary text where all that matters is what at first makes no sense and astonishes, the mirror effects, voids and flaws of these installations create stupor. In order to understand the *Nonsites*, one must try to read them, stratum after stratum, going back-and-forth between what is arranged within the delimited framework of the interior spaces, what is represented on the walls of the gallery on the one hand and the place of origin—distant, normally invisible, because it is fallow—of the different materials on the other.

One of the works that best sums up Smithson's subversive poetics is *The Museum of the Void* (1966-1968). The quick sketch, typical for the artist, shows a

RIGHT Robert Smithson, *The Museum of the Void*, 1966, ©Holt/Smithson Foundation/ VAGA at ARS, New York; Robert Smithson, *Island Project*, 1970, ©Holt/Smithson Foundation/ VAGA at ARS, New York

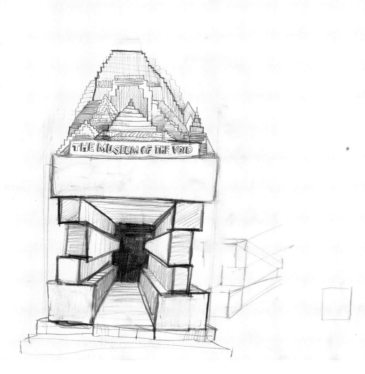

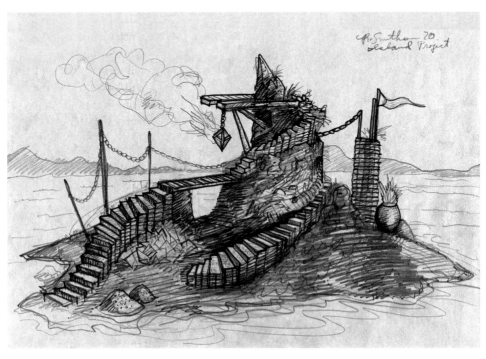

huge building made of large blocks and surmounted by a Piranesian collage of architectural elements ranging from the ziggurat to the pyramid. We have seen that the mountain/mound/pile/heap sign appears in Smithson as an expression of civilization that never ceases to erect, to pile up, to stack, to move things. Although already present in biological processes, such an activity leaves clear marks on the surface of the earth, sometimes forming "holes" of all kinds (upside down mountains), and sometimes "mountains," that is pits, quarries, mounds. By erecting mounds himself, by moving masses on a large scale, and organizing actions reminiscent of waste disposal, Smithson both imitates and deconstructs these processes linked to what we consider civilization. His Emmen mountain, *Spiral Hill*, devoid of any usefulness and added to a site beyond any economic logic, allows nevertheless a better understanding of what is really happening in a post-industrial society. Similarly, the exposed strata and sediments present in *The Museum of the Void* and in other works call for a critical interpretation of reality, a reading of the faults, ruptures, and intervals that dislocate the apparently compact matter that surrounds us.

The museum appears in this context as a particularly relevant place to continue this kind of critical reflection. The museum is, especially in the western tradition to which it is intimately linked, the essential institution capable of formulating the official reading of what is considered valuable. Conceived as institutions that favor order, museums are constantly amassing, accumulating, stacking. On a symbolic level, the museum thus resembles a mountain: it is the museum, intended as the summit of society, which contains the vestiges that really matter, and it is the museum that explains the order of things, including that of nature. By working far from the museum, in the immense wastelands of the polluted areas of the USA, or by bypassing the art gallery's urban insularity, Smithson clearly indicates his refusal of this institution. He even identifies it as a senseless place ("with no meaning") that would blind the visitor rather than enlighten him. However, his sketch of the *Museum of the Void* is both—and this is a characteristic of the artist—a parody of the museum and the vision of a different museum. On the parody side, we can see how this anti-museum tackles the impetus and immoderation of an institution that intends to ascend to the sky, defining along the way the place of everything worthy of being considered a major cultural product. One can imagine the museum institution in this perspective as an enormous mountain, systematically erected from the 19th century onwards, a container which reserves the "right" place for all the works considered as representative. With the *Museum of the Void* Smithson foresees the possibility of another form of the museum, an architecture of culture that would leave room for emptiness, doubts, and contradictions, instead of imposing at all costs the logic of identity and the "natural" place that would belong to this or that artistic work. The confused *bric-a-brac* on the roof of his *Museum of the Void* can thus be read in both directions: it could take the form

of everything large and exemplary, according to the "laws" of culture in force, but one can also think of a form of non-hierarchical architectural and artistic ruins, piled up at the top, in which the supreme part of this mountain-building simply would serve as a dumping ground. Smithson leaves, furthermore, a large void inside the building, a space that could potentially be filled over time and according to criteria to be defined. Is this a museum project? A model or an exercise in style? Is Smithson thinking of a museum with ruins, or rather of the ruins of a museum? The question is not settled, and this indecision and polysemy are a major characteristic of Smithson's work.[8] This is also what distinguishes him from the artists who worked with the mountain form in the same years and afterwards. Mark Tobin, for example, creates mountains that mimic termite mounds (*Termite Hills*, 2001); Giuseppe Penone has created among others a mound of potatoes (*Patate*, 1997); Wolfgang Laib designed tiny pollen mounds (*Die fünf unbesteigbaren Berge*, 1984); The painters Andrés Moya and Riccardo Taiana have masterfully reproduced mounds of garbage; Not Vital carved simulated mountains in plaster or marble (*Piz Nair*, 2011) and marble; etc. Many architects have also chosen the mountain as the main element for projects, particularly in the context of major international exhibitions. The case of Robert Smithson is, however, as we have shown, quite particular, because it eludes any rapid generalization. Two other major projects allow us to better understand the lasting relevance of his thought.

The first project, which was never completed because of Smithson's death in 1973, was thought for what is still today one of the largest man-made holes dug on the surface of the earth. The Bingham Copper Mine, still in operation, has mined since the 19th century a huge lava crust containing, among other

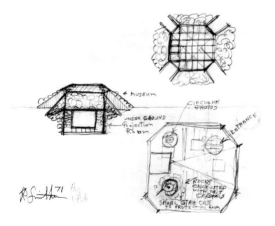

things, gold and copper. Based on a spiralic descent, this open pit mine forms a succession of terraces that is reminiscent of the conical architecture of a Dantesque hell, an upside-down mountain. At a time when "reclamation," the compensatory repair of heavily polluted industrial sites was already being demanded rather loud and clear, the Kennecott Mining Company had even imagined filling the gigantic 3-mile-wide funnel and thus hiding all traces of human intervention. In order to make such a large-scale undertaking happen, it would have become necessary to dismantle another mountain and spend more than thirty years to complete the repair work. In his visionary sketch Smithson thought, on the contrary, to safeguard the mark of the "wound" inflicted on the earth. The spiral terraces, leading ever lower, would have provided the sublime scenography for a de-escalation that culminated in the redeveloped center of the large hole. Smithson foresaw a huge disc spinning counterclockwise, or a lake transformed by the movement on its surface into a phenomenal "whirlpool." This vortex in the heart of the earth could have functioned as a powerful symbol and allowed us to understand the profound meaning of such a site. For the hollow mountain, explored through the nearly endless furrows is, in reality, only the negative form of all the material extracted, transported and used to build elsewhere. This time, by transposing the logic of the Nonsite (which in the art gallery was reminiscent of its distant and non-spectacular elsewhere) to a specific site, the mine, which in turn became a Nonsite, could have been reminiscent of the *elsewhere*, namely the positive topography it generated by providing an essential raw material for industry and construction. The gaping hole in Utah thus appears as the matrix of a constructive activity which, like the mine, at some point reaches its entropic limit. By not hiding anything and adding only the body of water—the support and symbol of reflection—, by making the void speak, Smithson saw here an extraordinary opportunity to create a highly effective anti-monument.

By questioning the mountain form, Smithson has always sought to avoid falling into the trap of the "perfect mountain,"[9] namely the presentation of a work, fabricated from scratch, which would give itself as definitive, absolute, smooth or ready to enter the museum. His most famous achievement, an icon of 20th century art, obeys this rule by decisively denying the idea of identity and completeness. *Spiral Jetty*—the huge jetty built in a heavily polluted salt lake at Rozel Point, Utah—has as its main characteristic that it is constantly changing over time. Depending on the water level of the lake, the spiral jetty emerges, rises or falls. It thus disappears for a period of time, metamorphoses into a rocky mass found below the surface, only to reappear again, later on, and "show" itself as an artificial topography. *Spiral Hill* and *Spiral Jetty* obviously have in common the theme of the entropic spiral. The flat anti-monument, built with extensive means on a site away from the inhabited world, represents, indeed, a subsequent variation on the theme of the artificial mountain. If one imagines the movement of the jetty in time, adding the temporal dimension to space, then this moving object turns out to be a huge pile of rocks that goes up and down. A dynamic 3D representation would provide an image of the *Spiral Jetty*'s verticality of the rocky mound. Its movement appears, in other words, as an upside-down representation of the geological processes that formed the earth's crust. In the manner of Emmen's spiral mountain, which serves as a vantage point for the *Broken Circle* and the post-industrial landscape, Smithson had imagined for his major work a construction that allows a different perspective. The museum designed for the *Spiral Jetty* (*Plan for a Museum Concerning Spiral Jetty*, 1971) would have added an additional layer and key to understanding the great jetty. The cavern-museum, resting on an octagonal base, would have been roughly covered on the outside with large blocks of basalt. The large room on the ground floor inside would have shown circular photos of the jetty. A spiral staircase, encrusted with salt, would have carried down to the "underground projection room." The "museum" therefore had to contain both outdoors and indoors, in a displaced manner, the material at the base of the *Spiral Jetty*: salt and rocks.

However, the essential was, once the visitor went downstairs, the contact with a Chthonian reality, which the show offered in the projection room. This "underground" location has several meanings: it refers to the topography of the projection location, but also to the form of the intended presentation. Smithson therefore thought (once his jetty had been built with enormous means, an object that sometimes completely escapes from view) of deconstructing his own work by making the visitor pass through a mountain-like deception of the cavern. Inside, the Spiral Jetty pilgrim could have discovered the representation of the work's difficult genesis thanks to photography first and then a film. Experimenting with the *Spiral Jetty* in this way would have set in motion an endless translation process, starting from the original on the surface, discovering the photographic version, below, later, and lower still, the film version. Upon leaving the Spiral Jetty Museum, the visitor could have rediscovered the external part, on the basis of the testimonials provided inside and so on, depending on the time available. Watching the film, which was intended to be the climax of the installation at Rozel Point, one realizes that it could have added to the immediate experience of the *Spiral Jetty* an essential reflexive and initiatory dimension. Any on site visit inevitably confronts the visitor with a stable and immobile state of the ensemble, whereas what really mattered to Smithson is, on the contrary, the idea of entropy, of flow and perpetual transformation. The visitor can only imagine a different state of the *Spiral Jetty* on the basis of the stories and documents, which the photographic and film documentation could have made available to him. Smithson's film, however, which he realized, goes much further. Its almost hypnotic structure that alternates over- and under-exposed shots is an exercise in non-representational logic. The rhythm of the first-person commentary also contributes to disturbing the viewer: "A muffled earthquake invades the floating tranquility, in a sensation of static rotation. The site was spinning, which locked itself in a huge curve. From this roundabout space emerged the idea of the Spiral Jetty."[10] Smithson spins both his object, the *Jetty*, and the viewer's head. At the culminating moment of the filmic journey, the "I" and its object seem to dissolve in a cosmic perspective: "The helicopter will maneuver in the reflection of the sun through the Spiral Jetty until it reaches its center. From this position, the fiery reflection evoked the source ion of a cyclotron that extended into a spiral of collapsed matter [...] All life seemed hesitant and stagnant [...] Was I something more than a shadow in a plastic bubble hovering in a place outside the mind and body? *Et in Utah Ego.* I was still slipping out of myself, dissolving into a single primary cell, trying to locate the nucleus at the end of the spiral."[11]

So here we are, at the end of an artistic journey which—while moving radically away from the values of the Disney-style cultural industry—uses the same means and the same methods used by the "society of the spectacle." The ultimate revelation of the *Spiral Jetty* would have taken place in a "cave cinema" reminding of an artificial mountain. The film that was supposed to explain the *Jetty* certainly turns towards the irrational, towards the space of imaginative freedom. The artist multiplies the "mental spirals" and proposes, from his "aerial" perspective, a form of fusion or final immersion in his work. Smithson, who had criticized the situation of the average moviegoer as a state close to "coma," exposes us to a state of consciousness that vertiginously approaches the point of dissolution.

What then remains of the critical potential of this work compared to the mechanisms of the society of the spectacle that it seems to denounce? Artificial mountains, heaps, jetties, islands and strata made by Smithson, are they ultimately just another form of what the master scenographers and the Imagineers, in agreement with the engineers, know to build so well? And what about their relationship with the logic of industrial and post-industrial production?

The answer to these questions has to be both positive and negative. On one hand, Smithson represents the opposite and a radical critique of the civilization of progress, engineering, electricity and image, a *Brunelleschian* civilization that was able to construct—on the basis of the concept of "design"—both the modern subject and the structured world that surrounds it. The unfinished, fluid and temporary nature of Smithson's projects clearly contradicts the hymns to progress and the values of the consumer society. Disney, Las Vegas (where, at the *Mirage Resort*, there is a fake volcano the size of a five-story building, with several "eruptions" a day) and their imitations around the world are characterized by a gigantic show devoid of any message. The entertainment industry is constantly erecting mountains whose "representations of the sublime and special effects were created only for entertainment. Their epiphanies have no referent; they reveal neither the existence of God, nor the power of nature, nor the greatness of human reason, but the titillations of self-representation."[12] Confronted with these expressions of the postmodern civilization of the spectacle, Smithson's works represent, on the contrary, a message in themselves through their strange, decontextualized, and unfinished quality (they obviously do not serve either to run the economy, it is "lost" money and energy). Even when they have become exemplary and the target of a form of postmodern artistic pilgrimage, these objects keep their marginality and leave their visitors perplexed. What do we see at Rozel Point if we only see the jetty? Or at Emmen, if you only see *Spiral Hill* and *Broken Circle*?

There is also no need to deny the structural resemblance between some purely spectacular artificial mountains and the artistic mountains built by Smithson. Both share the gigantism and the penchant for the technological sublime, as well as the omnipresent link to the universe of the machine. They represent the pinnacle of nature's staging, while at the same time being extremely artificial. Finally, they share the use of the most advanced techniques of representation and exist, on closer inspection, only through the images that precede them or that they never cease to generate.

The relationship of identity and difference that links the field of major exhibitions, theme parks and mountains of waste with Smithson's often anti-monumental and deliberately eccentric creations sheds a final light, based on the ambiguities suggested, on the path of our study.

One of the most important threads of this essay is the one which unites the spectacle, the architecture and the subject. The modern subject began, from the Renaissance onwards, to reconstruct Antiquity by erecting ambitious mounds. By building Parnassus, princes and their entourage occupied the horizon and sent powerful messages. The ephemeral mountain-shaped architectures, created by the artists of the Baroque period, were true machines of communication before the letter. Integrated into the great popular events of their time, they were becoming increasingly spectacular. The Revolution used the artificial mountain as a very effective means to convey key ideas. The "private" projects in Wörlitz and Branitz still follow this logic. The enormous mountain sign appears filled with different layers of meaning to be discovered by the erudite and amazed visitor. The era of the great exhibitions takes up this tradition by amplifying it in a hypertrophied way. Crowning the 1867 World Fair in Paris with the epiphanic appearance of a brand-new urban park that culminated in a mountain, built by rock workers and engineers, reflects the desire to express, thanks to a highly complex technological object, the control of the world claimed by the bourgeois subject. The utopia transposed by Bruno Taut into a new artificial landscape made it possible, at last, to use a chain of fake crystalline mountains as a programmatic message: by building a work of this scale, humanity would stop waging war (on itself). Even the scattered remains of the Second World War, scattered and gathered in the mountains of debris, were still *ex negativo* bearers of a message—namely the desire to conceal and forget the traces of the recent past.

The spectacular presence of the artificial mountain therefore appears, on one hand, as the material proof of the subject's rediscovered greatness. The mastery of its edification—of its structure, its solidity, its program, and its location—forms at the same time the mental space of a subject who, by constructing, was constructing himself. By increasingly controlling the assembly of the artificial mountain (symbolically: of the world), however, the projecting subject risked, on the other hand, being overwhelmed by the objects he had designed. Constructing disproportionate artifacts exposes the subject, in other words, to the danger of being manipulated by these same artifacts. The society of the postindustrial and postmodern spectacle marks both the triumph of the subject and the moment of its dissolution. At the end of the journey and in a situation where everything has become a spectacle, the artificial mountain devours the subject that built it. The subject disappears into its supreme artifact and dissolves, with paradoxical pleasure, as Robert Smithson, flying over his own work at Rozel Point, so aptly suggests: "Solids are only particles that organize themselves around a flow, they are only objective illusions supporting grains of dust, a collection of surfaces ready to break up."[13]

The path outlined in this essay based on a selection of specific artifacts is not to be confused with a teleological reconstruction. The hopes of the Renaissance and the project idea of this now-distant era is not only shattered in the light of modern events. The Renaissance was already in crisis ("broken," Smithson would say) and the modern age—although marked by increasingly deadly wars and the senseless exploitation of nature—still believes, in spite of everything, in a possible reemerging Renaissance.

The shadow that the artificial mountains of the 20th century cast on the past, therefore, allows us to sketch the elements of an anthropology rather than a historical development. This anthropology, found in the folds of the history of the artificial mountain, is based, inter alia, on the analogy existing between the state of the subject and the state of the earth, in the sign of the melancholy of the *Exegi monumentum* type, the man who constructs monuments that wither in spite of their apparent solidity. Digging to build, building here creating problems elsewhere, emptying to fill, move, pile up, etc., all these activities have completely changed the surface of the world, especially after the industrial revolution. In light of the few artificial mountains presented during our brief itinerary, the current state of the world is characterized by the existence of countless human-made mountains of all kinds and, above all, mountains of waste or industrial remains. In this context, one of the lessons to be learned from Robert Smithson's work is that of questioning the picturesque recycling of such cumbersome objects. From the perspective of the American artist and European tradition, which dominated the world until the 20th century, favored picturesque practices intended to mask the increasingly massive transformations of the industrial era. The Buttes-Chaumont, for example, appeared as a pseudo-nature skillfully erected to make people forget the "piercing" of Paris and, more generally, the tearing of the earth's surface, mechanically exploited in the service of progress. It is therefore understandable why Smithson admired Central Park, Olmsted's masterpiece, considering it as a gigantic machine rather than just a picturesque urban garden.

Another important conclusion that emerges from our journey and the critical reflection to which it is exposed (especially through Robert Smithson's works), is the key importance of representation. Extracting matter, piling up matter, giving matter a form, building, constructing, deconstructing, reconstructing, and finally, moving back and forth incessantly between these poles, namely the hollow and the full. All this is accompanied by processes privileging representation. Along the way, we encountered artificial mountains representing concepts (the distant Parnassus, the European nations, the Supreme Being), scientific ideas or personal destiny. Although self-referential, the Buttes-Chaumont also represented an idea (that of progress) and skills (those of engineers), a situation, which will continue in major national and international exhibitions.

With mounds of all kinds of waste, on one hand, and the artificial mountains of the theme park type, on the other, the starting point is different: while the former ostensibly represents nothing and escape all representation (they seem to escape the attention, photography, documentation), the latter have nothing to say because of their narcissistic self-referentiality. On one hand, then, the "nothing" of waste, heaps, mute mountains—an almost unknown "nothing" that nevertheless looks at us closely, since all these objects have indeed occupied the earth—and on the other hand, the "nothing" of the simulacrum, of false self-referential mountains, of hyper-known attractions. At a time when these two phenomena continue to advance—the Disneyland-type artificial mountain represents a state of the world under the banner of extreme standardization that culminates in the piling up of the banal, the architecture of non-places—the only instance that seems to support them is art. Smithson's works, but also those of all artists fascinated by the artificial mountain form and its topicality, represent the consciousness that, settling in the midst of these extremes, begins to speak, to take a stand and to point in another direction.

This form of attention also manifests itself in a memorable film by the Hungarian director Béla Tarr. *Kárhozat* (*Damnation*) tells the story of a lonely character, Karrer, who, when not wandering in a depressing moor, spends his time between his gloomy home and a bar, also sordid, the Titanik. The plot is as banal as its protagonists or the objects filmed. It is marked by small intrigues, and also desire, betrayed love, hatred, despair. What transcends however, the mundane melancholy suggested by Béla Tarr is the majestic shooting. It transforms the bodies and gestures of the actors into evocative signs, it is she who gives the landscapes—true other protagonists of Kárhozat—a special magic. However, the film begins with a very long traveling shot that shows Karrer sitting at the window watching a funicular for industrial use. Ignoring everything about the origin and purpose of the movement of transport materials, we are nevertheless witnessing a world in action. The end of the film, no less emblematic, sees Karrer wandering in an industrial wasteland not better identified. Moving between piles of debris, Karrer here literally behaves like a dog, barking at the real dog who is interested in him. As the rain continues to fall, Karrer prowls between distinct heaps of material reminiscent of the bleak universe of certain Antonioni or Tarkovsky films, until he completely disappears. The final sequence lingers for a long time on a mound of earth. Here, the artificial mountain has properly swallowed its subject.

ABOVE Béla Tarr, *Kárhozat*, 1988

1 Robert Smithson, *The Collected Writings*, University of California Press 1996, p. 216.

2 *Ibid.*, p. 240 (translated by the author).

3 See Rosalind Krauss, *Sculpture in the Expanded Field*, in: *October* 8 (1979), pp. 16-44: 30.

4 "And then you have just the piece. The piece is at once solidly there, but it is subject to the elements. And yet, all the battering they take, and as parts break off... the trickles and the bleeds on the side might disintegrate, the main body of it will just sort of lie there. I'm interested in that downslope." (Smithson, *op. cit.*, p. 215).

5 *Ibid.*, p. 87.

6 Robert Smithson, *A heap of language*.

7 "My thoughts are like an avalanche in the mind." (Smithson, *op. cit.*, p. 202)

8 From yet another perspective, the artist states: "For me, the world is a museum." (*Ibid.*, p. 246).

9 *Ibid.*, p. 203.

10 *Ibid.*, p. 206.

11 *Ibid.*, p. 149.

12 David E. Nye, *American Technological Sublime*, MIT Press, Cambridge Mass. 1994, p. 291.

13 Smithson, *The Collected Writings*, *op. cit.*, p. 107.

Acknowledgments

The present essay has benefited from the lectures I gave at the University of Luxembourg, the Weitzmann School of Design (University of Pennsylvania), Princeton, ETSAM (Madrid), IAAC (Barcelona), at the *Institut Européen des jardins et des paysages* (Bénouville), in Feltre, Arc-et-Senans, at the Politecnico di Milano, and at the Accademia di Architettura in Mendrisio.

The exhibition *Mountains and the Rise of Landscape*, which I curated in 2019 at the Graduate School of Design (Harvard), served as a test case for many aspects of my research.

I would like to thank, in a special way and in various capacities, Caroline Böttcher, Stéphanie de Courtois, Yolaine Escande, Marcello Fagiolo, Nicolas Fiévé, Monique Mosser, Philippe Neeser, Denis Ribouillault, Ada Segre, and Paola Sturla.

In memory of Gianquinto Perissinotto